SCIENTIFIC AMERICAN™
CUTTING-EDGE SCIENCE

Extreme Physics

New York

Published in 2008 by The Rosen Publishing Group, Inc.
29 East 21st Street, New York, NY 10010

The articles in this book first appeared in the pages of *Scientific American*, as follows: "Negative Energy, Wormholes and Warp Drive" by Lawrence H. Ford and Thomas A. Roman, January 2000; "Quantum Teleportation" by Anton Zeilinger, April 2000; "Parallel Universes" by Max Tegmark, May 2003; "Information in the Holographic Universe" by Jacob D. Bekenstein, August 2003; "The Future of String Theory: A Conversation with Brian Greene" by George Musser, November 2003; "Atoms of Space and Time" by Lee Smolin, January 2004; "The Dawn of Physics Beyond the Standard Model" by Gordon Kane, June 2003.

First Edition

Library of Congress Cataloging-in-Publication Data

Extreme physics.—1st ed.
     p. cm.—(Scientific American cutting-edge science)
Includes index.
ISBN-13: 978-1-4042-1406-4 (library binding)
1. Cosmology. 2. Quantum theory. 3. String models. 4. Particle physics.
I. Scientific American.
QB981.E98 2008
539—dc22
                                                                    2007028500

Manufactured in Singapore

On the cover: Illustration of quantum dice.

Illustration credits: Cover Alfred T. Kamajian; pp. 10, 12, 16, 17, 23 Michael Goodman; pp. 31, 38, 40, 44, 49 Laurie Grace; pp. 36, 37 David Fierstein; pp. 58, 64 (sphere), 70, 71, 79 (a–d), 93, 98 (top), 100, 103, 108 Alfred T. Kamajian; p. 61 (sphere) Max Tegmark; pp. 59 (square), 61, 64 (graphs), 65, 98 (graph) Sara Chen; p. 79 (earth's orbit) Bryan Christie; p. 113 Randy Harris; p. 122 Nova; pp. 152, 153, 155 Bryan Christie Design; p. 158 Nina Finkel.

Table of Contents

Introduction

Time travel, teleportation, parallel universes—in certain sectors of the physics community, notions once relegated to the realm of science fiction are now considered quite plausible. Indeed, by some accounts, the truth may be stranger than fiction. Consider the possibility that the universe is a huge hologram or that matter is composed of tiny, vibrating strings. Perhaps space and time are not continuous but instead come in discrete pieces. These are the wonderfully weird ways in which theorists are beginning to conceive of the world (or worlds!) around us.

In this book, leading authorities share their expertise on these cutting-edge ideas. Brian Greene untangles string theory; Max Tegmark reveals how astronomical observations support the existence of parallel universes; other scholars tackle quantum teleportation, negative energy, the holographic principle and loop quantum gravity; and Gordon Kane ushers in the dawn of physics beyond the Standard Model. —*The Editors*

I. "Negative Energy, Wormholes and Warp Drive"

by Lawrence H. Ford and Thomas A. Roman

The construction of wormholes and warp drive would require a very unusual form of energy. Unfortunately, the same laws of physics that allow the existence of this "negative energy" also appear to limit its behavior.

Can a region of space contain less than nothing? Common sense would say no; the most one could do is remove all matter and radiation and be left with vacuum. But quantum physics has a proven ability to confound intuition, and this case is no exception. A region of space, it turns out, can contain less than nothing. Its energy per unit volume—the energy density—can be less than zero.

Needless to say, the implications are bizarre. According to Einstein's theory of gravity, general relativity, the presence of matter and energy warps the geometric fabric of space and time. What we perceive as gravity is the space-time distortion produced by normal, positive energy or mass. But when negative energy or mass—so-called exotic matter—bends space-time, all sorts of amazing phenomena might become possible: traversable wormholes, which could act as tunnels to otherwise distant parts of the universe; warp drive, which would allow for faster-than-light travel; and time machines, which might permit journeys into the past. Negative energy could even be used to make perpetual-motion machines or to destroy black holes. A *Star Trek* episode could not ask for more.

For physicists, these ramifications set off alarm bells. The potential paradoxes of backward time travel— such as killing your grandfather before your father is conceived—have long been explored in science fiction, and the other consequences of exotic matter are also problematic. They raise a question of fundamental importance: Do the laws of physics that permit negative energy place any limits on its behavior? We and others have discovered that nature imposes stringent constraints on the magnitude and duration of negative energy, which (unfortunately, some would say) appear to render the construction of wormholes and warp drives very unlikely.

Double Negative

Before proceeding further, we should draw the reader's attention to what negative energy is not. It should not be confused with antimatter, which has positive energy. When an electron and its antiparticle, a positron, collide, they annihilate. The end products are gamma rays, which carry positive energy. If antiparticles were composed of negative energy, such an interaction would result in a final energy of zero. One should also not confuse negative energy with the energy associated with the cosmological constant, postulated in inflationary models of the universe [see "Cosmological Antigravity," by Lawrence M. Krauss; *Scientific American*, January

1999]. Such a constant represents negative pressure but positive energy. (Some authors call this exotic matter; we reserve the term for negative energy densities.)

The concept of negative energy is not pure fantasy; some of its effects have even been produced in the laboratory. They arise from Heisenberg's uncertainty principle, which requires that the energy density of any electric, magnetic or other field fluctuate randomly. Even when the energy density is zero on average, as in a vacuum, it fluctuates. Thus, the quantum vacuum can never remain empty in the classical sense of the term; it is a roiling sea of "virtual" particles spontaneously popping in and out of existence [see "Exploiting Zero-Point Energy," by Philip Yam; *Scientific American*, December 1997]. In quantum theory, the usual notion of zero energy corresponds to the vacuum with all these fluctuations. So if one can somehow contrive to dampen the undulations, the vacuum will have less energy than it normally does—that is, less than zero energy.

As an example, researchers in quantum optics have created special states of fields in which destructive quantum interference suppresses the vacuum fluctuations. These so-called squeezed vacuum states involve negative energy. More precisely, they are associated with regions of alternating positive and negative energy. The total energy averaged over all space remains positive; squeezing the vacuum creates negative energy in one place at the price of extra positive energy elsewhere. A typical experiment involves laser beams passing through nonlinear optical materials [see "Squeezed Light," by

Richart E. Slusher and Bernard Yurke; *Scientific American*, May 1988]. The intense laser light induces the material to create pairs of light quanta, photons. These photons alternately enhance and suppress the vacuum fluctuations, leading to regions of positive and negative energy, respectively.

Another method for producing negative energy introduces geometric boundaries into a space. In 1948 Dutch physicist Hendrik B. G. Casimir showed that two uncharged parallel metal plates alter the vacuum fluctuations in such a way as to attract each other. The energy density between the plates was later calculated to be negative. In effect, the plates reduce the fluctuations in the gap between them; this creates negative energy and pressure, which pulls the plates together. The narrower the gap, the more negative the energy and pressure, and the stronger is the attractive force. The Casimir effect has recently been measured by Steve K. Lamoreaux of Los Alamos National Laboratory and by Umar Mohideen of the University of California at Riverside and his colleague Anushree Roy. Similarly, in the 1970s Paul C. W. Davies and Stephen A. Fulling, then at King's College at the University of London, predicted that a moving boundary, such as a moving mirror, could produce a flux of negative energy.

For both the Casimir effect and squeezed states, researchers have measured only the indirect effects of negative energy. Direct detection is more difficult but might be possible using atomic spins, as Peter G.

Grove, then at the British Home Office, Adrian C. Ottewill, then at the University of Oxford, and one of us (Ford) suggested in 1992.

Gravity and Levity

The concept of negative energy arises in several areas of modern physics. It has an intimate link with black holes, those mysterious objects whose gravitational field is so strong that nothing can escape from within their boundary, the event horizon. In 1974 Stephen W. Hawking of the University of Cambridge made his famous prediction that black holes evaporate by emitting radiation [see "The Quantum Mechanics of Black Holes," by Stephen W. Hawking; *Scientific American*, January 1977]. A black hole radiates energy at a rate inversely proportional to the square of its mass. Although the evaporation rate is large only for subatomic-size black holes, it provides a crucial link between the laws of black holes and the laws of thermodynamics. The Hawking radiation allows black holes to come into thermal equilibrium with their environment.

At first glance, evaporation leads to a contradiction. The horizon is a one-way street; energy can only flow inward. So how can a black hole radiate energy outward? Because energy must be conserved, the production of positive energy—which distant observers see as the Hawking radiation—is accompanied by a flow of negative energy into the hole. Here the negative energy is produced by the extreme space-time curvature near the

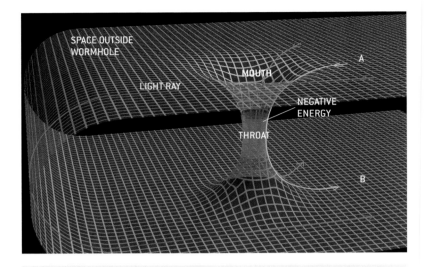

Wormhole acts as a tunnel between two different locations in space. Light rays from A to B can enter one mouth of the wormhole, pass through the throat and exit at the other mouth—a journey that would take much longer if they had to go the long way around. At the throat must be negative energy, whose gravitational field allows converging light rays to begin diverging. (This diagram is a two-dimensional representation of three-dimensional space. The mouths and throat of the wormhole are actually spheres.) Although not shown here, a wormhole could also connect two different points in time.

hole, which disturbs the vacuum fluctuations. In this way, negative energy is required for the consistency of the unification of black hole physics with thermodynamics.

The black hole is not the only curved region of space-time where negative energy seems to play a role. Another is the wormhole—a hypothesized type of tunnel that connects one region of space and time to another. Physicists used to think that wormholes exist only on the very finest length scales, bubbling in and out of existence like virtual particles [see "Quantum Gravity," by Bryce S. DeWitt; *Scientific American*, December 1983]. In the early 1960s physicists Robert Fuller and John A. Wheeler showed that larger wormholes would collapse under their own gravity so rapidly that even a beam of light would not have enough time to travel through them.

But in the late 1980s various researchers—notably Michael S. Morris and Kip S. Thorne of the California Institute of Technology and Matt Visser of Washington University—found otherwise. Certain wormholes could in fact be made large enough for a person or spaceship. Someone might enter the mouth of a wormhole stationed on Earth, walk a short distance inside the wormhole and exit the other mouth in, say, the Andromeda galaxy. The catch is that traversable wormholes require negative energy. Because negative energy is gravitationally repulsive, it would prevent the wormhole from collapsing.

For a wormhole to be traversable, it ought to (at bare minimum) allow signals, in the form of light rays, to pass through it. Light rays entering one mouth of a wormhole are converging, but to emerge from the other mouth, they must defocus—in other words, they must go from converging to diverging somewhere in between [see illustration on page 10]. This defocusing requires negative energy. Whereas the curvature of space produced by the attractive gravitational field of ordinary matter acts like a converging lens, negative energy acts like a diverging lens.

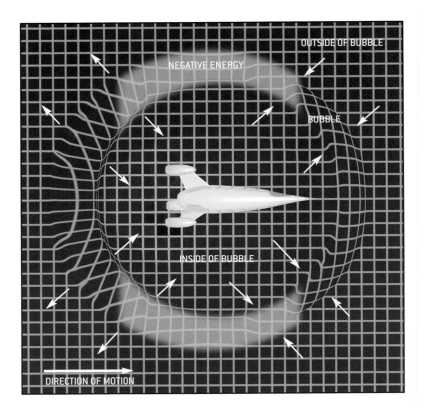

Space-time bubble is the closest that modern physics comes to the "warp drive" of science fiction. It can convey a starship at arbitrarily high speeds. Space-time contracts at the front of the bubble, reducing the distance to the destination, and expands at its rear, increasing the distance from the origin (*arrows*). The ship itself stands still relative to the space immediately around it; crew members do not experience any acceleration. Negative energy is required on the sides of the bubble.

No Dilithium Needed

Such space-time contortions would enable another staple of science fiction as well: faster-than-light travel. In 1994 Miguel Alcubierre Moya, then at the University of Wales at Cardiff, discovered a solution to Einstein's equations that has many of the desired features of warp drive. It describes a space-time bubble that transports a starship at arbitrarily high speeds relative to observers outside the bubble. Calculations show that negative energy is required.

Warp drive might appear to violate Einstein's special theory of relativity. But special relativity says that you cannot outrun a light signal in a fair race in which you and the signal follow the same route. When space-time is warped, it might be possible to beat a light signal by taking a different route, a shortcut. The contraction of space-time in front of the bubble and the expansion behind it create such a shortcut [see "Space-Time Bubble" illustration].

One problem with Alcubierre's original model, pointed out by Sergei V. Krasnikov of the Central Astronomical Observatory at Pulkovo near St. Petersburg, is that the interior of the warp bubble is causally disconnected from its forward edge. A starship captain on the inside cannot steer the bubble or turn it on or off; some external agency must set it up ahead of time. To get around this problem, Krasnikov proposed a "superluminal subway," a tube of modified space-time (not the same as a wormhole) connecting Earth and a distant star. Within the tube, superluminal travel in one direction is possible. During the outbound journey at sublight speed, a spaceship crew would create such a tube. On the return journey, they could travel through it at warp speed. Like warp bubbles, the subway involves negative energy. It has since been shown by Ken D. Olum of Tufts University and by Visser, together with Bruce Bassett of Oxford and Stefano Liberati of the International School for Advanced Studies in Trieste, that any scheme for faster-than-light travel requires the use of negative energy.

If one can construct wormholes or warp drives, time travel might become possible. The passage of time is relative; it depends on the observer's velocity. A person who leaves Earth in a spaceship, travels at near lightspeed and returns will have aged less than someone who remains on Earth. If the traveler manages to outrun a light ray, perhaps by taking a shortcut through a wormhole or a warp bubble, he may return before he left. Morris, Thorne and Ulvi Yurtsever, then at Caltech, proposed a wormhole time machine in 1988, and their paper has stimulated much research on time travel over the past decade. In 1992 Hawking proved that any construction of a time machine in a finite region of space-time inherently requires negative energy.

Negative energy is so strange that one might think it must violate some law of physics. Before and after the creation of equal amounts of negative and positive energy in previously empty space, the total energy is zero, so the law of conservation of energy is obeyed. But there are many phenomena that conserve energy yet never occur in the real world. A broken glass does not reassemble itself, and heat does not spontaneously flow from a colder to a hotter body. Such effects are forbidden by the second law of thermodynamics. This general principle states that the degree of disorder of a system—its entropy—cannot decrease on its own without an input of energy. Thus, a refrigerator, which pumps heat from its cold interior to the warmer outside room, requires an external power source. Similarly, the second law also forbids the complete conversion of heat into work.

Negative energy potentially conflicts with the second law. Imagine an exotic laser, which creates a steady outgoing beam of negative energy. Conservation of energy requires that a by-product be a steady stream of positive energy. One could direct the negative energy beam off to some distant corner of the universe, while employing the positive energy to perform useful work. This seemingly inexhaustible energy supply could be used to make a perpetual-motion machine and thereby violate the second law. If the beam were directed at a glass of water, it could cool the water while using the extracted positive energy to power a small motor— providing a refrigerator with no need for external power. These problems arise not from the existence of negative energy per se but from the unrestricted separation of negative and positive energy.

View from the bridge of a faster-than-light starship as it heads in the direction of the Little Dipper (*above*) looks nothing like the star streaks typically depicted in science fiction. As the velocity increases, stars ahead of the ship (*facing page, left column*) appear ever closer to the direction of motion and turn bluer in color. Behind the ship (*facing page, right column*), stars shift closer to a position directly astern, redden and eventually disappear from view altogether. The light from stars directly overhead or underneath remains unaffected.

Unfettered negative energy would also have profound consequences for black holes. When a black hole forms by the collapse of a dying star, general relativity predicts the formation of a singularity, a region where the gravitational field becomes infinitely strong. At this point, general relativity—and indeed all known laws of physics—are unable to say what happens next. This inability is a profound failure of the current

FORWARD VIEW REAR VIEW

SHIP AT REST

10 TIMES LIGHTSPEED

100 TIMES LIGHTSPEED

mathematical description of nature. So long as the singularity is hidden within an event horizon, however, the damage is limited. The description of nature everywhere outside of the horizon is unaffected. For this reason, Roger Penrose of Oxford proposed the cosmic censorship hypothesis: there can be no naked singularities, which are unshielded by event horizons.

For special types of charged or rotating black holes—known as extreme black holes—even a small increase in charge or spin, or a decrease in mass, could in principle destroy the horizon and convert the hole into a naked singularity. Attempts to charge up or spin up these black holes using ordinary matter seem to fail for a variety of reasons. One might instead envision producing a decrease in mass by shining a beam of negative energy down the hole, without altering its charge or spin, thus subverting cosmic censorship. One might create such a beam, for example, using a moving mirror. In principle, it would require only a tiny amount of negative energy to produce a dramatic change in the state of an extreme black hole. Therefore, this might be the scenario in which negative energy is the most likely to produce macroscopic effects.

Not Separate and Not Equal

Fortunately (or not, depending on your point of view), although quantum theory allows the existence of negative energy, it also appears to place strong restrictions—

known as quantum inequalities—on its magnitude and duration. These inequalities were first suggested by Ford in 1978. Over the past decade they have been proved and refined by us and others, including Éanna E. Flanagan of Cornell University, Michael J. Pfenning, then at Tufts, Christopher J. Fewster and Simon P. Eveson of the University of York, and Edward Teo of the National University of Singapore.

The inequalities bear some resemblance to the uncertainty principle. They say that a beam of negative energy cannot be arbitrarily intense for an arbitrarily long time. The permissible magnitude of the negative energy is inversely related to its temporal or spatial extent. An intense pulse of negative energy can last for a short time; a weak pulse can last longer. Furthermore, an initial negative energy pulse must be followed by a larger pulse of positive energy [see "View from the Bridge" illustration]. The larger the magnitude of the negative energy, the nearer must be its positive energy counterpart. These restrictions are independent of the details of how the negative energy is produced. One can think of negative energy as an energy loan. Just as a debt is negative money that has to be repaid, negative energy is an energy deficit. As we will discuss below, the analogy goes even further.

In the Casimir effect, the negative energy density between the plates can persist indefinitely, but large negative energy densities require a very small plate separation. The magnitude of the negative energy density is inversely proportional to the fourth power of the plate separation. Just as a pulse with a very negative energy density is limited in time, very negative Casimir energy density must be confined between closely spaced plates. According to the quantum inequalities, the energy density in the gap can be made more negative than the Casimir value, but only temporarily. In effect, the more one tries to depress the energy density below the Casimir value, the shorter the time over which this situation can be maintained.

When applied to wormholes and warp drives, the quantum inequalities typically imply that such structures must either be limited to submicroscopic sizes, or if they are macroscopic the negative energy must be confined to incredibly thin bands. In 1996 we showed that a submicroscopic wormhole would have a throat radius of no more than about 10^{-32} meter. This is only slightly larger than the Planck length, 10^{-35} meter, the smallest distance that has definite meaning. We found that it is possible to have models of wormholes of macroscopic size but only at the price of confining the negative energy to an extremely thin band around the throat. For example, in one model a throat radius of 1 meter requires the negative energy to be a band no thicker than 10^{-21} meter, a millionth the size of a proton. Visser has estimated that the negative energy required for this size of wormhole has a magnitude equivalent to the total energy generated by 10 billion stars in one year. The situation does not improve much for larger wormholes. For the same model, the maximum allowed thickness of the negative energy band is proportional to the cube root of the throat radius. Even if the throat radius is increased to a size of one light-year, the negative energy must still be confined to a region smaller than a proton radius, and the total amount required increases linearly with the throat size.

It seems that wormhole engineers face daunting problems. They must find a mechanism for confining large amounts of negative energy to extremely thin volumes. So-called cosmic strings, hypothesized in some cosmological theories, involve very large energy densities in long, narrow lines. But all known physically reasonable cosmic-string models have positive energy densities.

Warp drives are even more tightly constrained, as shown by Pfenning and Allen Everett of Tufts, working with us. In Alcubierre's model, a warp bubble traveling at 10 times lightspeed (warp factor 2, in the parlance of *Star Trek: The Next Generation*) must have a wall thickness of no more than 10^{-32} meter. A bubble large enough to enclose a starship 200 meters across would require a total amount of negative energy equal to 10 billion times the mass of the observable universe. Similar constraints apply to Krasnikov's superluminal subway. A modification of Alcubierre's model was recently constructed by Chris Van Den Broeck of the Catholic University of Louvain in Belgium. It requires much less negative energy but places the starship in a curved space-time bottle whose neck is about 10^{-32} meter across, a difficult feat. These results would seem to make it rather unlikely that one could construct wormholes and warp drives using negative energy generated by quantum effects.

Cosmic Flashing and Quantum Interest

The quantum inequalities prevent violations of the second law. If one tries to use a pulse of negative energy to cool a hot object, it will be quickly followed by a larger pulse of positive energy, which reheats the object. A weak pulse of negative energy could remain separated from its positive counterpart for a longer time, but its effects would be indistinguishable from normal thermal fluctuations. Attempts to capture or split off negative energy from positive energy also appear to fail. One might intercept an energy beam, say, by using a box with a shutter. By closing the shutter, one might hope to trap a pulse of negative energy before the offsetting positive energy arrives. But the very act of closing the shutter creates an energy flux that cancels out the negative energy it was designed to trap [see "Attempt to Circumvent" illustration].

We have shown that there are similar restrictions on violations of cosmic censorship. A pulse of negative energy injected into a charged black hole might momentarily destroy the horizon, exposing the singularity within. But the pulse must be followed by a pulse

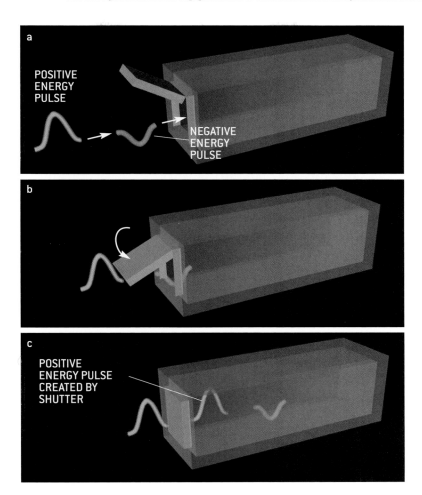

a

POSITIVE
ENERGY
PULSE

NEGATIVE
ENERGY
PULSE

b

c

POSITIVE
ENERGY PULSE
CREATED BY
SHUTTER

Attempt to circumvent the quantum laws that govern negative energy inevitably ends in disappointment. The experimenter intends to detach a negative energy pulse from its compensating positive energy pulse. As the pulses approach a box (a), the experimenter tries to isolate the negative one by closing the lid after it has entered (b). Yet the very act of closing the lid creates a second positive energy pulse inside the box (c).

of positive energy, which would convert the naked singularity back into a black hole—a scenario we have dubbed cosmic flashing. The best chance to observe cosmic flashing would be to maximize the time separation between the negative and positive energy, allowing the naked singularity to last as long as possible. But then the magnitude of the negative energy pulse would have to be very small, according to the quantum inequalities. The change in the mass of the black hole caused by the negative energy pulse will get washed out by the normal quantum fluctuations in the hole's mass, which are a natural consequence of the uncertainty principle. The view of the naked singularity would thus be blurred, so a distant observer could not unambiguously verify that cosmic censorship had been violated.

Recently we, and also Frans Pretorius, then at the University of Victoria, and Fewster and Teo, have shown that the quantum inequalities lead to even stronger bounds on negative energy. The positive pulse that necessarily follows an initial negative pulse must do more than compensate for the negative pulse; it must overcompensate. The amount of overcompensation increases with the time interval between the pulses. Therefore, the negative and positive pulses can never be made to exactly cancel each other. The positive energy must always dominate—an effect known as quantum interest. If negative energy is thought of as an energy loan, the loan must be repaid with interest. The longer the loan period or the larger the loan amount, the greater is the interest. Furthermore, the larger the loan, the smaller is the maximum allowed loan period. Nature is a shrewd banker and always calls in its debts.

The concept of negative energy touches on many areas of physics: gravitation, quantum theory, thermodynamics. The interweaving of so many different parts of physics illustrates the tight logical structure of the laws of nature. On the one hand, negative energy seems to be required to reconcile black holes with thermodynamics. On the other, quantum physics prevents unrestricted production of negative energy, which would violate the second law of thermodynamics. Whether these restrictions are also features of some deeper underlying theory, such as quantum gravity, remains to be seen. Nature no doubt has more surprises in store.

Further Information

Black Holes and Time Warps: Einstein's Outrageous Legacy. Kip S. Thorne. W. W. Norton, 1994.

Lorentzian Wormholes: From Einstein to Hawking. Matt Visser. American Institute of Physics Press, 1996.

Quantum Field Theory Constrains Traversable Wormhole Geometries. L. H. Ford and T. A. Roman in Physical Review D, Vol. 53, No. 10, pages 5496–5507; May 15, 1996. Available at xxx.lanl.gov/abs/gr-qc/9510071 on the World Wide Web.

The Unphysical Nature of Warp Drive. M. J. Pfenning and L. H. Ford in *Classical and Quantum Gravity*, Vol. 14, No. 7, pages 1743–1751; July 1997. Available at **xxx.lanl.gov/abs/gr-qc/9702026** on the World Wide Web.

Paradox Lost. Paul Davies in *New Scientist*, Vol. 157, No. 2126, page 26; March 21, 1998.

Time Machines: Time Travel in Physics, Metaphysics, and Science Fiction. Second edition. Paul J. Nahin. AIP Press, Springer-Verlag, 1999.

The Quantum Interest Conjecture. L. H. Ford and T. A. Roman in *Physical Review* D, Vol. 60, No. 10, Article No. 104018 (8 pages); November 15, 1999. Available at **xxx.lanl.gov/abs/gr-qc/9901074** on the World Wide Web.

About The Authors

LAWRENCE H. FORD and THOMAS A. ROMAN have collaborated on negative energy issues for over a decade. Ford received his Ph.D. from Princeton University in 1974, working under John Wheeler, one of the founders of black hole physics. He is now a professor of physics at Tufts University and works on problems in both general relativity and quantum theory, with a special interest in quantum fluctuations. His other pursuits include hiking in the New England woods and gathering wild mushrooms. Roman received his Ph.D. in 1981 from Syracuse University under Peter Bergmann, who collaborated with Albert Einstein on unified field theory. Roman has been a frequent visitor at the Tufts Institute of Cosmology during the past 10 years and is currently a professor of physics at Central Connecticut State University. His interests include the implications of negative energy for a quantum theory of gravity. He tends to avoid wild mushrooms.

2. "Quantum Teleportation"

By Anton Zeilinger

The science-fiction dream of "beaming" objects from place to place is now a reality—at least for particles of light.

The scene is a familiar one from science-fiction movies and TV: an intrepid band of explorers enters a special chamber; lights pulse, sound effects warble, and our heroes shimmer out of existence to reappear on the surface of a faraway planet. This is the dream of teleportation—the ability to travel from place to place without having to pass through the tedious intervening miles accompanied by a physical vehicle and airline-food rations. Although the teleportation of large objects or humans still remains a fantasy, quantum teleportation has become a laboratory reality for photons, the individual particles of light.

Quantum teleportation exploits some of the most basic (and peculiar) features of quantum mechanics, a branch of physics invented in the first quarter of the 20th century to explain processes that occur at the level of individual atoms. From the beginning, theorists realized that quantum physics led to a plethora of new phenomena, some of which defy common sense. Technological progress in the final quarter of the 20th century has enabled researchers to conduct many experiments that not only demonstrate fundamental, sometimes bizarre aspects of quantum mechanics but, as in the case of quantum teleportation, apply them to achieve previously inconceivable feats.

In science-fiction stories, teleportation often permits travel that is instantaneous, violating the speed limit set down by Albert Einstein, who concluded from his theory of relativity that nothing can travel faster than light. Teleportation is also less cumbersome than the more ordinary means of space travel. It is said that Gene Roddenberry, the creator of *Star Trek*, conceived of the "transporter beam" as a way to save the expense of simulating landings and takeoffs on strange planets.

The procedure for teleportation in science fiction varies from story to story but generally goes as follows: A device scans the original object to extract all the information needed to describe it. A transmitter sends the information to the receiving station, where it is used to obtain an exact replica of the original. In some cases, the material that made up the original is also transported to the receiving station, perhaps as "energy" of some kind; in other cases, the replica is made of atoms and molecules that were already present at the receiving station.

Quantum mechanics seems to make such a tele-portation scheme impossible in principle. Heisenberg's uncertainty principle rules that one cannot know both the precise position of an object and its momentum at the same time. Thus, one cannot perform a perfect scan of the object to be teleported; the location or velocity of every atom and electron would be subject to errors. Heisenberg's uncertainty principle also applies to other pairs of quantities, making it impossible to measure the exact, total quantum state of any object with certainty. Yet such measurements would be necessary to obtain all the information needed to describe the original exactly. (In *Star Trek* the "Heisenberg Compensator" somehow miraculously overcomes that difficulty.)

A team of physicists overturned this conventional wisdom in 1993, when they discovered a way to use quantum mechanics itself for teleportation. The team— Charles H. Bennett of IBM; Gilles Brassard, Claude Crépeau and Richard Josza of the University of Montreal; Asher Peres of Technion–Israel Institute of Technology; and William K. Wootters of Williams College—found that a peculiar but fundamental feature of quantum mechanics, entanglement, can be used to circumvent the limitations imposed by Heisenberg's uncertainty principle without violating it.

Entanglement

It is the year 2100. A friend who likes to dabble in physics and party tricks has brought you a collection of pairs of dice. He lets you roll them once, one pair at a time. You handle the first pair gingerly, remembering the fiasco with the micro–black hole last Christmas. Finally, you roll the two dice and get double 3. You roll the next pair. Double 6. The next: double 1. They always match.

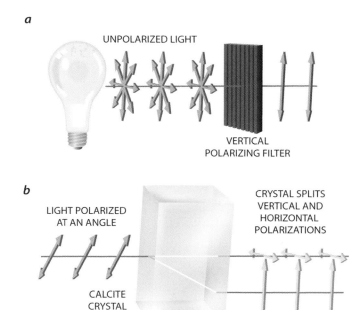

a

UNPOLARIZED LIGHT

VERTICAL
POLARIZING FILTER

b

LIGHT POLARIZED
AT AN ANGLE

CRYSTAL SPLITS
VERTICAL AND
HORIZONTAL
POLARIZATIONS

CALCITE
CRYSTAL

Unpolarized light consists of photons that are polarized in all directions (*a*). In polarized light the photons' electric-field oscillations (*arrows*) are all aligned. A calcite crystal (*b*) splits a light beam in two, sending photons that are polarized parallel with its axis into one beam and those that are perpendicular into the other. Intermediate angles go into a quantum superposition of both beams. Each such photon can be detected in one beam or the other, with probability depending on the angle. Because probabilities are involved, we cannot measure the unknown polarization of a single photon with certainty.

The dice in this fable are behaving as if they were quantum entangled particles. Each die on its own is random and fair, but its entangled partner somehow always gives the correct matching outcome. Such behavior has been demonstrated and intensively studied with real entangled particles. In typical experiments, pairs of atoms, ions or photons stand in for the dice, and properties such as polarization stand in for the different faces of a die.

Consider the case of two photons whose polarizations are entangled to be random but identical. Beams of light and even individual photons consist of oscillations of electromagnetic fields, and polarization refers to the alignment of the electric field oscillations [see "Unpolarized Light" illustration]. Suppose that Alice has one of the entangled photons and Bob has its partner. When Alice measures her photon to see if it is horizontally or vertically polarized, each outcome has a 50 percent chance. Bob's photon has the same probabilities, but the entanglement ensures that he will get exactly the same result as Alice. As soon as Alice gets the result "horizontal," say, she knows that Bob's photon will also be horizontally polarized. Before Alice's measurement the two photons do not have individual polarizations; the entangled state specifies only that a measurement will find that the two polarizations are equal.

An amazing aspect of this process is that it doesn't matter if Alice and Bob are far away from each other; the process works so long as their photons' entanglement has been preserved. Even if Alice is on Alpha Centauri and Bob on Earth, their results will agree when they compare them. In every case, it is as if Bob's photon is magically influenced by Alice's distant measurement, and vice versa.

You might wonder if we can explain the entanglement by imagining that each particle carries within it
some recorded instructions. Perhaps when we entangle
the two particles, we synchronize some hidden mechanism within them that determines what results they
will give when they are measured. This would explain
away the mysterious effect of Alice's measurement on
Bob's particle. In the 1960s, however, Irish physicist
John Bell proved a theorem that in certain situations
any such "hidden variables" explanation of quantum
entanglement would have to produce results different
from those predicted by standard quantum mechanics.
Experiments have confirmed the predictions of quantum
mechanics to a very high accuracy.

Austrian physicist Erwin Schrödinger, one of the
co-inventors of quantum mechanics, called entanglement
"the essential feature" of quantum physics. Entanglement
is often called the EPR effect and the particles EPR pairs,
after Einstein, Boris Podolsky and Nathan Rosen, who
in 1935 analyzed the effects of entanglement acting
across large distances. Einstein talked of it as "spooky
action at a distance." If one tried to explain the results
in terms of signals traveling between the photons, the
signals would have to travel faster than the speed of
light. Naturally, many people have wondered if this
effect could be used to transmit information faster than
the speed of light.

Unfortunately, the quantum rules make that impossible. Each local measurement on a photon, considered
in isolation, produces a completely random result and so

can carry no information from the distant location. It tells you nothing more than what the distant measurement result probabilities would be, depending on what was measured there. Nevertheless, we can put entanglement to work in an ingenious way to achieve quantum teleportation.

Putting Entangled Photons to Work

Alice and Bob anticipate that they will want to teleport a photon in the future. In preparation, they share an entangled auxiliary pair of photons, Alice taking photon A and Bob photon B. Instead of measuring them, they each store their photon without disturbing the delicate entangled state.

In due course, Alice has a third photon—call it photon X—that she wants to teleport to Bob. She does not know what photon X's state is, but she wants Bob to have a photon with that same polarization. She cannot simply measure the photon's polarization and send Bob the result. In general, her measurement result would not be identical to the photon's original state. This is Heisenberg's uncertainty principle at work.

Instead, to teleport photon X, Alice measures it jointly with photon A, without determining their individual polarizations. She might find, for instance, that their polarizations are "perpendicular" to each other (she still does not know the absolute polarization of either one, however). Technically, the joint measurement of photon A and photon X is called a Bell-state measurement. Alice's measurement produces a subtle effect: it changes Bob's photon to correlate with a combination of her measurement result and the state that photon X originally had. In fact, Bob's photon now carries her photon X's state, either exactly or modified in a simple way.

To complete the teleportation, Alice must send a message to Bob—one that travels by conventional means, such as a telephone call or a note on a scrap of paper. After he receives this message, if necessary Bob can transform his photon B, with the end result that it becomes an exact replica of the original photon X. Which transformation Bob must apply depends on the outcome of Alice's measurement. There are four possibilities, corresponding to four quantum relations between her photons A and X. A typical transformation that Bob must apply to his photon is to alter its polarization by 90 degrees, which he can do by sending it through a crystal with the appropriate optical properties.

Which of the four possible results Alice obtains is completely random and independent of photon X's original state. Bob therefore does not know how to process his photon until he learns the result of Alice's measurement. One can say that Bob's photon instantaneously contains all the information from Alice's original, transported there by quantum mechanics. Yet to know how to read that information, Bob must

Preparing for Quantum Teleportation

Quantum teleportation of a person (impossible in practice but a good example to aid the imagination) would begin with the person inside a measurement chamber (*left*) alongside an equal mass of auxiliary material. The auxiliary matter has previously been quantum-entangled with its counterpart, which is at the faraway receiving station (*right*).

A Quantum Measurement

Joint measurement carried out on the auxiliary matter and the person (*left*) changes them to a random quantum state and produces a vast amount of random (but significant) data—two bits per elementary state. By "spooky action at a distance," the measurement also instantly alters the quantum state of the faraway counterpart matter (*right*).

Transmission of Random Data

Measurement data must be sent to the distant receiving station by conventional means. This process is limited by the speed of light, making it impossible to teleport the person faster than the speed of light.

Reconstruction of the Traveler

Receiver re-creates the traveler, exact down to the quantum state of every atom and molecule, by adjusting the counterpart matter's state according to the random measurement data sent from the scanning station.

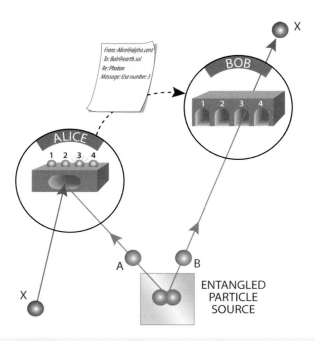

From: Alice@alpha.cent
To: Bob@earth.sol
Re: Photon
Message: Use number 3

Ideal quantum teleportation relies on Alice, the sender, and Bob, the receiver, sharing a pair of entangled particles A and B. Alice has a particle that is in an unknown quantum state X. Alice performs a Bell-state measurement on particles A and X, producing one of four possible outcomes. She tells Bob about the result by ordinary means. Depending on Alice's result, Bob leaves his particle unaltered (1) or rotates it (2, 3, 4). Either way it ends up a perfect replica of the original particle X.

wait for the classical information, consisting of two bits that can travel no faster than the speed of light.

Skeptics might complain that the only thing teleported is the photon's polarization state or, more generally, its quantum state, not the photon "itself." But because a photon's quantum state is its defining characteristic, teleporting its state is completely equivalent to teleporting the particle [see "Skeptics Corner" box].

Note that quantum teleportation does not result in two copies of photon X. Classical information can be copied any number of times, but perfect copying of quantum information is impossible, a result known as the no-cloning theorem, which was proved by Wootters and Wojciech H. Zurek of Los Alamos National Laboratory in 1982. (If we could clone a quantum state, we could use the clones to violate Heisenberg's principle.) Alice's measurement actually entangles her photon A with photon X, and photon X loses all memory, one might say, of its original state. As a member of an entangled pair, it has no individual polarization state. Thus, the original state of photon X disappears from Alice's domain.

Circumventing Heisenberg

Furthermore, photon X's state has been transferred to Bob with neither Alice nor Bob learning anything about what the state is. Alice's measurement result, being entirely random, tells them nothing about the state. This is how the process circumvents Heisenberg's principle, which stops us from determining the complete quantum state of a particle but does not preclude teleporting the complete state so long as we do not try to see what the state is!

photon passing through a special crystal sometimes generates two new photons that are entangled so that they will show opposite polarization when measured.

A much more difficult problem is to entangle two independent photons that already exist, as must occur during the operation of a Bell-state analyzer. This means that the two photons (A and X) somehow have to lose their private features. In 1997 my group (Dik Bouwmeester, Jian-Wei Pan, Klaus Mattle, Manfred Eibl and Harald Weinfurter), then at the University of Innsbruck, applied a solution to this problem in our teleportation experiment [see "Innsbruck Experiment" illustration].

In our experiment, a brief pulse of ultraviolet light from a laser passes through a crystal and creates the entangled photons A and B. One travels to Alice, and the other goes to Bob. A mirror reflects the ultraviolet pulse back through the crystal again, where it may create another pair of photons, C and D. (These will also be entangled, but we don't use their entanglement.) Photon C goes to a detector, which alerts us that its partner D is available to be teleported. Photon D passes through a polarizer, which we can orient in any conceivable way. The resulting polarized photon is our photon X, the one to be teleported, and travels on to Alice. Once it passes through the polarizer, X is an independent photon, no longer entangled. And although *we* know its polarization because of how we set the polarizer, Alice does not. We reuse the same ultraviolet pulse in this way to ensure that Alice has photons A and X at the same time.

Now we arrive at the problem of performing the Bell-state measurement. To do this, Alice combines her two photons (A and X) using a semireflecting mirror, a device that reflects half of the incident light. An individual photon has a 50–50 chance of passing through or being reflected. In quantum terms, the photon goes into a superposition of these two possibilities [see "Beam Splitter" illustration].

Now suppose that two photons strike the mirror from opposite sides, with their paths aligned so that the reflected path of one photon lies along the transmitted path of the other, and vice versa. A detector waits at the end of each path. Ordinarily the two photons would be reflected independently, and there would be a 50 percent chance of them arriving in separate detectors. If the photons are indistinguishable and arrive at the mirror at the same instant, however, quantum interference takes place: some possibilities cancel out and do not occur, whereas others reinforce and occur more often. When the photons interfere, they have only a 25 percent likelihood of ending up in separate detectors. Furthermore, when that occurs it corresponds to detecting one of the four possible Bell states of the two photons—the case that we called "lucky" earlier. The other 75 percent of the time the two photons both end up in one detector, which corresponds to the other three Bell states but does not discriminate among them.

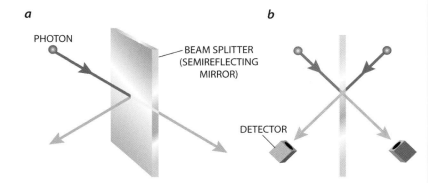

Beam splitter, or semireflecting mirror (*a*), reflects half the light that hits it and transmits the other half. An individual photon has a 50–50 chance of reflection or transmission. If two identical photons strike the beam splitter at the same time, one from each side (*b*), the reflected and transmitted parts interfere, and the photons lose their individual identities. We will detect one photon in each detector 25 percent of the time, and it is then impossible to say if both photons were reflected or both were transmitted. Only the relative property—that they went to different detectors—is measured.

When Alice simultaneously detects one photon in each detector, Bob's photon instantly becomes a replica of Alice's original photon X. We verified that this teleportation occurred by showing that Bob's photon had the polarization that we imposed on photon X. Our experiment was not perfect, but the correct polarization was detected 80 percent of the time (random photons would achieve 50 percent). We demonstrated the procedure with a variety of polarizations: vertical, horizontal, linear at 45 degrees and even a nonlinear kind of polarization called circular polarization.

The most difficult aspect of our Bell-state analyzer is making photons A and X indistinguishable. Even the timing of when the photons arrive could be used to identify which photon is which, so it is important to "erase" the time information carried by the particles. In our experiment, we used a clever trick first suggested by Marek Zukowski of the University of Gdansk: we send the photons through very narrow bandwidth wavelength filters. This process makes the wavelength of the photons very precise, and by Heisenberg's uncertainty relation it smears out the photons in time.

A mind-boggling case arises when the teleported photon was itself entangled with another and thus did not have its own individual polarization. In 1998 my Innsbruck group demonstrated this scenario by giving Alice photon D without polarizing it, so that it was still entangled with photon C. We showed that when the teleportation succeeded, Bob's photon B ended up entangled with C. Thus, the *entanglement* with C had been transmitted from A to B.

Piggyback States

Our experiment clearly demonstrated teleportation, but it had a low rate of success. Because we could identify just one Bell state, we could teleport Alice's photon only 25 percent of the time—the occasions when that state occurred. No complete Bell-state analyzer exists for independent photons or for any two independently

Skeptics Corner
The Author Answers Common Teleportation Questions

Isn't it an exaggeration to call this teleportation? After all, it is only a quantum state that is teleported, not an actual object.

This question raises the deeper philosophical one of what we mean by identity. How do we know that an object— say, the car we find in our garage in the morning—is the same one we saw a while ago? When it has all the right features and properties. Quantum physics reinforces this point: particles of the same type in the same quantum state are indistinguishable even in principle. If one could carefully swap all the iron atoms in the car with those from a lump of ore and reproduce the atoms' states exactly, the end result would be identical, at the deepest level, to the original car. Identity cannot mean more than this: being the same in all properties.

Isn't it more like "quantum faxing"?

Faxing produces a copy that is easy to tell apart from the original, whereas a teleported object is indistinguishable even in principle. Moreover, in quantum teleportation the original must be destroyed.

Can we really hope to teleport a complicated object?

There are many severe obstacles. First, the object has to be in a pure quantum state, and such states are very fragile. Photons don't interact with air much, so our experiments can be done in the open, but experiments with atoms and larger objects must be done in a vacuum to avoid collisions with gas molecules. Also, the larger an object becomes, the easier it is to disturb its quantum state. A tiny lump of matter would be disturbed even by thermal radiation from the walls of the apparatus. This is why we do not routinely see quantum effects in our everyday world.

Quantum interference, an easier effect to produce than entanglement or teleportation, has been demonstrated with buckyballs, spheres made of 60 carbon atoms. Such work will proceed to larger objects, perhaps even small viruses, but don't hold your breath for it to be repeated with full-size soccer balls!

Another problem is the Bell-state measurement. What would it mean to do a Bell-state measurement of a virus consisting of, say, 10^7 atoms? How would we extract the 10^8 bits of information that such a measurement would generate? For an object of just a few grams the numbers become impossible: 10^{24} bits of data.

Would teleporting a person require quantum accuracy?

Being in the same quantum state does not seem necessary for being the same person. We change our states all the time and remain the same people—at least as far as we can tell! Conversely, identical twins or biological clones are not "the same people," because they have different memories. Does Heisenberg uncertainty prevent us from replicating a person precisely enough for her to think she was the same as the original? Who knows. It is intriguing, however, that the quantum no-cloning theorem prohibits us from making a perfect replica of a person.

created quantum particles, so at present there is no experimentally proven way to improve our scheme's efficiency to 100 percent.

In 1994 a way to circumvent this problem was proposed by Sandu Popescu, then at the University of Cambridge. He suggested that the state to be teleported could be a quantum state riding piggy-back on Alice's auxiliary photon A. Francesco De Martini's group at the University of Rome I "La Sapienza" successfully demonstrated this scheme in 1997. The auxiliary pair of photons was entangled according to the photons' locations: photon A was split, as by a beam splitter, and sent to two different parts of Alice's apparatus, with the two alternatives linked by entanglement to a similar splitting of Bob's photon B. The state to be teleported was also carried by Alice's photon A—its polarization state. With both roles played by one photon, detecting all four possible Bell states becomes a standard single-particle measurement: detect Alice's photon in one of two possible locations with one of two possible polarizations. The drawback of the scheme is that if Alice were given a separate unknown state X to be teleported she would somehow have to transfer the state onto the polarization of her photon A, which no one knows how to do in practice.

Polarization of a photon, the feature employed by the Innsbruck and the Rome experiments, is a discrete quantity, in that any polarization state can be expressed as a superposition of just two discrete states, such as vertical and horizontal polarization. The electromagnetic field associated with light also has continuous features that amount to superpositions of an infinite number of basic states. For example, a light beam can be "squeezed," meaning that one of its properties is made extremely precise or noise-free, at the expense of greater randomness in another property (à la Heisenberg). In 1998 Jeffrey Kimble's group at the California Institute of Technology teleported such a squeezed state from one beam of light to another, thus demonstrating teleportation of a continuous feature.

Remarkable as all these experiments are, they are a far cry from quantum teleportation of large objects. There are two essential problems: First, one needs an entangled pair of the same kind of objects. Second, the object to be teleported and the entangled pairs must be sufficiently isolated from the environment. If any information leaks to or from the environment through stray interactions, the objects' quantum states degrade, a process called decoherence. It is hard to imagine how we could achieve such extreme isolation for a large piece of equipment, let alone a living creature that breathes air and radiates heat. But who knows how fast development might go in the future?

Certainly we could use existing technology to teleport elementary states, like those of the photons in our experiment, across distances of a few kilometers and maybe even up to satellites. The technology to

Quantum Computers

Perhaps the most realistic application of quantum teleportation outside of pure physics research is in the field of quantum computation. A conventional digital computer works with bits, which take definite values of 0 or 1, but a quantum computer uses quantum bits, or qubits [see "Quantum Computing with Molecules," by Neil Gershenfeld and Issac L. Chuang, *Scientific American*, June 1998] Qubits can be in quantum superpositions of 0 and 1 just as a photon can be in a superposition of horizontal and vertical polarization. Indeed, in sending a single photon, the basic quantum teleporter transmits a single qubit of quantum information.

Superpositions of numbers may seem strange, but as the late Rolf Landauer of IBM put it, "When we were little kids learning to count on our very sticky classical fingers, we didn't know about quantum mechanics and superposition. We gained the wrong intuition. We thought that information was classical. We thought that we could hold up three fingers, then four. We didn't realize that there could be a superposition of both."

A quantum computer can work on a superposition of many different inputs at once. For example, it could run an algorithm simultaneously on one million inputs, using only as many qubits as a conventional computer would need bits to run the algorithm once on a single input. Theorists have proved that algorithms running on quantum computers can solve certain problems faster (that is, in fewer computational steps) than any known algorithm running on a classical computer can. The problems include finding items in a database and factoring large numbers, which is of great interest for breaking secret codes.

So far only the most rudimentary elements of quantum computers have been built: logic gates that can process one or two qubits. The realization of even a small-scale quantum computer is still far away. A key problem is transferring quantum data reliably between different logic gates or processors, whether within a single quantum computer or across quantum networks. Quantum teleportation is one solution.

In addition, Daniel Gottesman of Microsoft and Isaac L. Chuang of IBM recently proved that a general-purpose quantum computer can be built out of three basic components: entangled particles, quantum teleporters and gates that operate on a single qubit at a time. This result provides a systematic way to construct two-qubit gates. The trick of building a two-qubit gate from a teleporter is to teleport two qubits from the gate's input to its output, using carefully modified entangled pairs. The entangled pairs are modified in just such a way that the gate's output receives the appropriately processed qubits. Performing quantum logic on two unknown qubits is thus reduced to the tasks of preparing specific predefined entangled states and teleporting. Admittedly, the complete Bell-state measurement needed to teleport with 100 percent success is itself a type of two-qubit processing. —A. Z.

teleport states of individual atoms is at hand today: the group led by Serge Haroche at the École Normale Supérieure in Paris has demonstrated entanglement of atoms. The entanglement of molecules and then their teleportation may reasonably be expected within the next decade. What happens beyond that is anybody's guess.

A more important application of teleportation might very well be in the field of quantum computation, where the ordinary notion of bits (0's and 1's) is generalized to quantum bits, or qubits, which can exist as super-positions and entanglements of 0's and 1's. Teleportation could be used to transfer quantum information between quantum processors. Quantum teleporters can also serve as basic components used to build a quantum computer.

Quantum mechanics is probably one of the profoundest theories ever discovered. The problems that it poses for our everyday intuition about the world led Einstein to criticize quantum mechanics very strongly. He insisted that physics should be an attempt to grasp a reality that exists independently of its observation. Yet he realized that we run into deep problems when we try to assign such an independent physical reality to the individual members of an entangled pair. His great counterpart, Danish physicist Niels Bohr, insisted that one has to take into account the whole system—in the case of an entangled pair, the arrangement of both particles together. Einstein's desideratum, the independent real state of each particle, is devoid of meaning for an entangled quantum system.

Quantum teleportation is a direct descendant of the scenarios debated by Einstein and Bohr. When we analyze the experiment, we would run into all kinds of problems if we asked ourselves what the properties of the individual particles *really* are when they are entangled. We have to analyze carefully what it means to "have" a polarization. We cannot escape the conclusion that all we can talk about are certain experimental results obtained by measurements. In our polarization measurement, a click of the detector lets us construct a picture in our mind in which the photon actually "had" a certain polarization at the time of measurement. Yet we must always remember that this is just a made-up story. It is valid only if we talk about that specific experiment, and we should be cautious in using it in other situations.

Indeed, following Bohr, I would argue that we can understand quantum mechanics if we realize that science is not describing how nature *is* but rather expresses what we can *say* about nature. This is where the current value of fundamental experiments such as teleportation lies: in helping us to reach a deeper understanding of our mysterious quantum world.

Further Information

Quantum Information and Computation. Charles H. Bennett in *Physics Today*, Vol. 48, No. 10, pages 24–31; October 1995.

Experimental Quantum Teleportation. D. Bouwmeester, J. W. Pan, K. Mattle, M. Eibl, H. Weinfurter and A. Zeilinger in *Nature*, Vol. 390, pages 575–579; December 11, 1997.

Quantum Information. Special issue of *Physics World*, Vol. 11, No. 3; March 1998.

Quantum Theory: Weird and Wonderful. A. J. Leggett in *Physics World*, Vol. 12, No. 12, pages 73–77; December 1999.

More about quantum teleportation and related physics experiments is available at **www.quantum** at on the World Wide Web.

The Author

ANTON ZEILINGER is at the Institute for Experimental Physics at the University of Vienna, having teleported there in 1999 after nine years at the University of Innsbruck. He considers himself very fortunate to have the privilege of working on exactly the mysteries and paradoxes of quantum mechanics that drew him into physics nearly 40 years ago. In his little free time, Zeilinger interacts with classical music and with jazz, loves to ski, and collects antique maps.

3. "Parallel Universes"

By Max Tegmark

Not just a staple of science fiction, other universes are a direct implication of cosmological observations.

Is there a copy of you reading this article? A person who is not you but who lives on a planet called Earth, with misty mountains, fertile fields and sprawling cities, in a solar system with eight other planets? The life of this person has been identical to yours in every respect. But perhaps he or she now decides to put down this article without finishing it, while you read on.

The idea of such an alter ego seems strange and implausible, but it looks as if we will just have to live with it, because it is supported by astronomical observations. The simplest and most popular cosmological model today predicts that you have a twin in a galaxy about 10 to the 10^{28} meters from here. This distance is so large that it is beyond astronomical, but that does not make your doppelgänger any less real. The estimate is derived from elementary probability and does not even assume speculative modern physics, merely that space is infinite (or at least sufficiently large) in size and almost uniformly filled with matter, as observations indicate. In infinite space, even the most unlikely events must take place somewhere. There are infinitely many other inhabited planets, including not just one but infinitely many that have people with the same appearance, name and memories as you, who play out every possible permutation of your life choices.

You will probably never see your other selves. The farthest you can observe is the distance that light has been able to travel during the 14 billion years since the big bang expansion began. The most distant visible objects are now about 4×10^{26} meters away—a distance that defines our observable universe, also called our Hubble volume, our horizon volume or simply our universe. Likewise, the universes of your other selves are spheres of the same size centered on their planets. They are the most straightforward example of parallel universes. Each universe is merely a small part of a larger "multiverse."

By this very definition of "universe," one might expect the notion of a multiverse to be forever in the domain of metaphysics. Yet the borderline between physics and metaphysics is defined by whether a theory is experimentally testable, not by whether it is weird or involves unobservable entities. The frontiers of physics have gradually expanded to incorporate ever more abstract (and once metaphysical) concepts such as a round Earth, invisible electromagnetic fields, time slowdown at high speeds, quantum superpositions, curved space, and black holes. Over the past several years the concept of a multiverse has joined this list. It is grounded in well-tested theories such as relativity and quantum mechanics, and it fulfills both of the basic criteria of an empirical science: it makes predictions, and it can be falsified. Scientists have discussed as many as four distinct types of parallel universes. The key question is not whether the multiverse exists but rather how many levels it has.

Level I: Beyond Our Cosmic Horizon

The parallel universes of your alter egos constitute the Level I multiverse. It is the least controversial type. We all accept the existence of things that we cannot see but could see if we moved to a different vantage point or merely waited, like people watching for ships to come over the horizon. Objects beyond the cosmic horizon have a similar status. The observable universe grows by a light-year every year as light from farther away has time to reach us. An infinity lies out there, waiting to be seen. You will probably die long before your alter egos come into view, but in principle, and if cosmic expansion cooperates, your descendants could observe them through a sufficiently powerful telescope.

If anything, the Level I multiverse sounds trivially obvious. How could space *not* be infinite? Is there a sign somewhere saying "Space Ends Here—Mind the Gap?" If so, what lies beyond it? In fact, Einstein's theory of gravity calls this intuition into question. Space could be finite if it has a convex curvature or an unusual topology (that is, interconnectedness). A spherical, doughnut-shaped or pretzel-shaped universe would have a limited volume and no edges. The cosmic microwave background radiation allows sensitive tests of such scenarios [see "Is Space Finite?" by Jean-Pierre Luminet, Glenn D. Starkman and Jeffrey R. Weeks; *Scientific American*, April 1999]. So far, however, the evidence is against them. Infinite models fit the data, and strong limits have been placed on the alternatives.

Another possibility is that space is infinite but matter is confined to a finite region around us—the historically popular "island universe" model. In a variant on this model, matter thins out on large scales in a fractal pattern. In both cases, almost all universes in the Level I multiverse would be empty and dead. But recent observations of the three-dimensional galaxy distribution and the microwave background have shown that the arrangement of matter gives way to dull uniformity on large scales, with no coherent structures larger than about 10^{24} meters. Assuming that

Overview: Multiverses

- One of the many implications of recent cosmological observations is that the concept of parallel universes is no mere metaphor. Space appears to be infinite in size. If so, then somewhere out there, everything that is possible becomes real, no matter how improbable it is. Beyond the range of our telescopes are other regions of space that are identical to ours. Those regions are a type of parallel universe. Scientists can even calculate how distant these universes are, on average.
- And that is fairly solid physics. When cosmologists consider theories that are less well established, they conclude that other universes can have entirely different properties and laws of physics. The presence of those universes would explain various strange aspects of our own. It could even answer fundamental questions about the nature of time and the comprehensibility of the physical world.

this pattern continues, space beyond our observable universe teems with galaxies, stars and planets.

Observers living in Level I parallel universes experience the same laws of physics as we do but with different initial conditions. According to current theories, processes early in the big bang spread matter around with a degree of randomness, generating all possible arrangements with nonzero probability. Cosmologists assume that our universe, with an almost uniform distribution of matter and initial density fluctuations of one part in 100,000, is a fairly typical one (at least among those that contain observers). That assumption underlies the estimate that your closest identical copy is 10 to the 10^{28} meters away. About 10 to the 10^{92} meters away, there should be a sphere of radius 100 light-years identical to the one centered here, so all perceptions that we have during the next century will be identical to those of our counterparts over there. About 10 to the 10^{118} meters away should be an entire Hubble volume identical to ours.

These are extremely conservative estimates, derived simply by counting all possible quantum states that a Hubble volume can have if it is no hotter than 10^8 kelvins. One way to do the calculation is to ask how many protons could be packed into a Hubble volume at that temperature. The answer is 10^{118} protons. Each of those particles may or may not, in fact, be present, which makes for 2 to the 10^{118} possible arrangements of protons. A box containing that many Hubble volumes exhausts all the possibilities. If you round off

Level I Multiverse

The simplest type of parallel universe is simply a region of space that is too far away for us to have seen yet. The farthest that we can observe is currently about 4×10^{26} meters, or 42 billion light-years—the distance that light has been able to travel since the big bang began. (The distance is greater than 14 billion light-years because cosmic expansion has lengthened distances.) Each of the Level I parallel universes is basically the same as ours. All the differences stem from variations in the initial arrangement of matter.

limit of observation

4×10^{26} meters

Our Universe

Parallel Universe

Parallel Universe

$10^{10^{115}}$ meters

Identical Parallel Universe

How Far Away Is a Duplicate Universe?

EXAMPLE UNIVERSE

Imagine a two-dimensional universe with space for four particles. Such a universe has 2^4, or 16, possible arrangements of matter. If more than 16 of these universes exist, they must begin to repeat. In this example, the distance to the nearest duplicate is roughly four times the diameter of each universe.

4 particles

2^4 arrangements

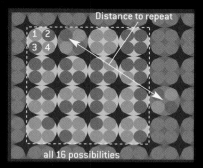

Distance to repeat

all 16 possibilities

OUR UNIVERSE

The same argument applies to our universe, which has space for about 10^{118} subatomic particles. The number of possible arrangements is therefore 2 to the 10^{118}, or approximately 10 to the 10^{118}. Multiplying by the diameter of the universe gives an average distance to the nearest duplicate of 10 to the 10^{118} meters.

2×10^{-13} meter

10^{118} particles

$2^{10^{118}}$ arrangement

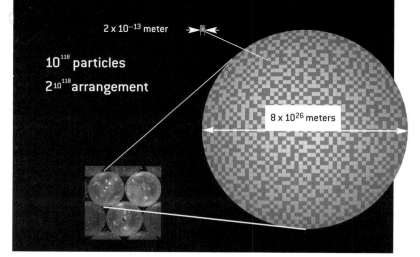

8×10^{26} meters

the numbers, such a box is about 10 to the 10^{118} meters across. Beyond that box, universes—including ours—must repeat. Roughly the same number could be derived by using thermodynamic or quantum-gravitational estimates of the total information content of the universe.

Your nearest doppelgänger is most likely to be much closer than these numbers suggest, given the processes of planet formation and biological evolution that tip the odds in your favor. Astronomers suspect that our Hubble volume has at least 10^{20} habitable planets; some might well look like Earth.

The Level I multiverse framework is used routinely to evaluate theories in modern cosmology, although this procedure is rarely spelled out explicitly. For instance, consider how cosmologists used the microwave background to rule out a finite spherical geometry. Hot and cold spots in microwave background maps have a characteristic size that depends on the curvature of space, and the observed spots appear too small to be consistent with a spherical shape. But it is important to be statistically rigorous. The average spot size varies randomly from one Hubble volume to another, so it is possible that our universe is fooling us—it could be spherical but happen to have abnormally small spots. When cosmologists say they have ruled out the spherical model with 99.9 percent confidence, they really mean that if this model were true, fewer than one in 1,000 Hubble volumes would show spots as small as those we observe.

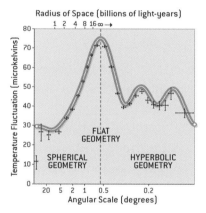

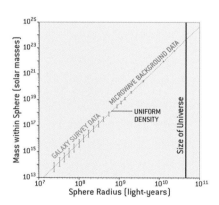

Cosmological data support the idea that space continues beyond the confines of our observable universe. The WMAP satellite recently measured the fluctuations in the microwave background (*left*). The strongest fluctuations are just over half a degree across, which indicates—after applying the rules of geometry—that space is very large or infinite (*center*). (One caveat: some cosmologists speculate that the discrepant point on the left of the graph is evidence for a finite volume.) In addition, WMAP and the 2dF Galaxy Redshift Survey have found that space on large scales is filled with matter uniformly (*right*), meaning that other universes should look basically like ours.

The lesson is that the multiverse theory can be tested and falsified even though we cannot see the other universes. The key is to predict what the ensemble of parallel universes is and to specify a probability distribution, or what mathematicians call a "measure," over that ensemble. Our universe should emerge as one of the most probable. If not—if, according to the multiverse theory, we live in an improbable universe—then the theory is in trouble. As I will discuss later, this measure problem can become quite challenging.

Level II: Other Postinflation Bubbles

If the level I multiverse was hard to stomach, try imagining an infinite set of distinct Level I multiverses, some perhaps with different spacetime dimensionality and different physical constants. Those other multiverses—which constitute a Level II multiverse—are predicted by the currently popular theory of chaotic eternal inflation.

Inflation is an extension of the big bang theory and ties up many of the loose ends of that theory, such as why the universe is so big, so uniform and so flat. A rapid stretching of space long ago can explain all these and other attributes in one fell swoop [see "The Inflationary Universe," by Alan H. Guth and Paul J. Steinhard; *Scientific American*, May 1984; and "The Self-Reproducing Inflationary Universe," by Andrei Linde, November 1994]. Such stretching is predicted by a wide class of theories of elementary particles, and all available evidence bears it out. The phrase "chaotic eternal" refers to what happens on the very largest scales. Space as a whole is stretching and will continue doing so forever, but some regions of space stop stretching and form distinct bubbles, like gas pockets in a loaf of rising bread. Infinitely many such bubbles emerge. Each is an embryonic Level I multiverse: infinite in size and filled with matter deposited by the energy field that drove inflation.

Those bubbles are more than infinitely far away from Earth, in the sense that you would never get there even if you traveled at the speed of light forever. The reason is that the space between our bubble and its neighbors is expanding faster than you could travel through it. Your descendants will never see their doppelgängers elsewhere in Level II. For the same reason, if cosmic expansion is accelerating, as observations now suggest, they might not see their alter egos even in Level I.

The Level II multiverse is far more diverse than the Level I multiverse. The bubbles vary not only in their initial conditions but also in seemingly immutable aspects of nature. The prevailing view in physics today is that the dimensionality of spacetime, the qualities of elementary particles and many of the so-called physical constants are not built into physical laws but are the outcome of processes known as symmetry breaking. For instance, theorists think that the space in our universe once had nine dimensions, all on an equal footing. Early in cosmic history, three of them partook in the cosmic expansion and became the three dimensions we now

Level II Multiverse

A somewhat more elaborate type of parallel universe emerges from the theory of cosmological inflation. The idea is that our Level I multiverse—namely, our universe and contiguous regions of space—is a bubble embedded in an even vaster but mostly empty volume. Other bubbles exist out there, disconnected from ours. They nucleate like raindrops in a cloud. During nucleation, variations in quantum fields endow each bubble with properties that distinguish it from other bubbles.

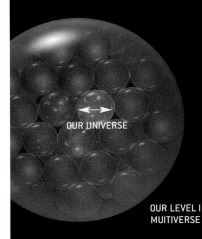

OUR UNIVERSE

Empty
Space
(INFLATING)

PARALLEL
LEVEL I
MUITIVERSE

OUR LEVEL I
MUITIVERSE

PARALLEL
LEVEL I
MUITIVERSE

Bubble Nucleation
A quantum field known as the inflaton causes space to expand rapidly. In the bulk of space, random fluctuations prevent the field from decaying away. But in certain regions, the field loses its strength and the expansion slows down. Those regions become bubbles.

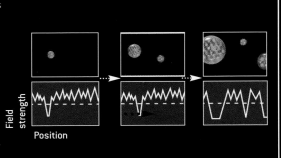

Field strength

Position

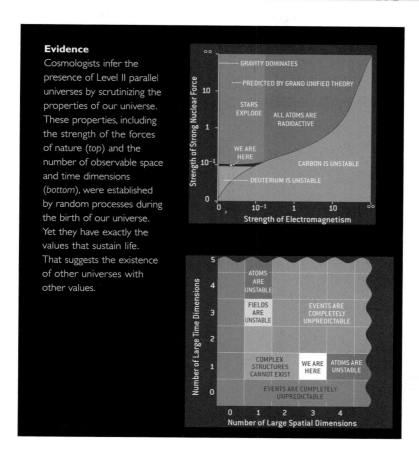

Evidence

Cosmologists infer the presence of Level II parallel universes by scrutinizing the properties of our universe. These properties, including the strength of the forces of nature (*top*) and the number of observable space and time dimensions (*bottom*), were established by random processes during the birth of our universe. Yet they have exactly the values that sustain life. That suggests the existence of other universes with other values.

observe. The other six are now unobservable, either because they have stayed microscopic with a doughnut-like topology or because all matter is confined to a three-dimensional surface (a membrane, or simply "brane") in the nine-dimensional space.

Thus, the original symmetry among the dimensions broke. The quantum fluctuations that drive chaotic inflation could cause different symmetry breaking in different bubbles. Some might become four-dimensional, others could contain only two rather than three generations of quarks, and still others might have a stronger cosmological constant than our universe does.

Another way to produce a Level II multiverse might be through a cycle of birth and destruction of universes. In a scientific context, this idea was introduced by physicist Richard C. Tolman in the 1930s and recently elaborated on by Paul J. Steinhardt of Princeton University and Neil Turok of the University of Cambridge. The Steinhardt and Turok proposal and related models involve a second three-dimensional brane that is quite literally parallel to ours, merely offset in a higher dimension [see "Been There, Done That," by George Musser; News Scan, *Scientific American*, March 2002]. This parallel universe is not really a separate universe, because it interacts with ours. But the ensemble of universes—past, present and future—that these branes create would form a multiverse, arguably with a diversity similar to that produced by chaotic inflation. An idea proposed by physicist Lee Smolin of the Perimeter Institute in Waterloo, Ontario, involves yet another multiverse comparable in diversity to that of Level II but mutating and sprouting new universes through black holes rather than through brane physics.

Although we cannot interact with other Level II parallel universes, cosmologists can infer their presence indirectly, because their existence can account for unexplained coincidences in our universe. To give an analogy, suppose you check into a hotel, are assigned room 1967 and note that this is the year you were born. What a coincidence, you say. After a moment of reflection, however, you conclude that this is not so surprising after all. The hotel has hundreds of rooms, and you would not have been having these thoughts in the first place if you had been assigned one with a number that meant nothing to you. The lesson is that even if you knew nothing about hotels, you could infer the existence of other hotel rooms to explain the coincidence.

As a more pertinent example, consider the mass of the sun. The mass of a star determines its luminosity, and using basic physics, one can compute that life as we know it on Earth is possible only if the sun's mass falls into the narrow range between 1.6×10^{30} and 2.4×10^{30} kilograms. Otherwise Earth's climate would be colder than that of present-day Mars or hotter than that of present-day Venus. The measured solar mass is 2.0×10^{30} kilograms. At first glance, this apparent coincidence of the habitable and observed mass values appears to be a wild stroke of luck. Stellar masses run from 10^{29} to 10^{32} kilograms, so if the sun acquired its mass at random, it had only a small chance of falling into the habitable range. But just as in the hotel example, one can explain this apparent coincidence by postulating an ensemble (in this case, a number of planetary systems) and a selection effect (the fact that we must find ourselves living on a habitable planet). Such observer-related selection effects are referred to as "anthropic," and although the "A-word" is notorious for triggering controversy, physicists broadly agree that these selection effects cannot be neglected when testing fundamental theories.

What applies to hotel rooms and planetary systems applies to parallel universes. Most, if not all, of the attributes set by symmetry breaking appear to be fine-tuned. Changing their values by modest amounts would have resulted in a qualitatively different universe—one in which we probably would not exist. If protons were 0.2 percent heavier, they could decay into neutrons, destabilizing atoms. If the electromagnetic force were 4 percent weaker, there would be no hydrogen and no normal stars. If the weak interaction were much weaker, hydrogen would not exist; if it were much stronger, supernovae would fail to seed interstellar space with heavy elements. If the cosmological constant were much larger, the universe would have blown itself apart before galaxies could form.

Although the degree of fine-tuning is still debated, these examples suggest the existence of parallel universes with other values of the physical constants [see "Exploring Our Universe and Others," by Martin Rees; *Scientific American*, December 1999]. The Level II multiverse theory predicts that physicists will never be able to determine the values of these constants from first principles. They will merely compute probability distributions for what they should expect to find, taking selection effects into account. The result should be as generic as is consistent with our existence.

Level III: Quantum Many Worlds

The Level I and Level II multiverses involve parallel worlds that are far away, beyond the domain even of astronomers. But the next level of multiverse is right around you. It arises from the famous, and famously controversial, many-worlds interpretation of quantum mechanics—the idea that random quantum processes cause the universe to branch into multiple copies, one for each possible outcome.

In the early 20th century the theory of quantum mechanics revolutionized physics by explaining the atomic realm, which does not abide by the classical rules of Newtonian mechanics. Despite the obvious successes of the theory, a heated debate rages about what it really means. The theory specifies the state of the universe not in classical terms, such as the positions and velocities of all particles, but in terms of a mathematical object called a wave function. According to the Schrödinger equation, this state evolves over time in a fashion that mathematicians term "unitary," meaning that the wave function rotates in an abstract infinite-dimensional space called Hilbert space. Although quantum mechanics is often described as inherently random and uncertain, the wave function

Level III Multiverse

Quantum mechanics predicts a vast number of parallel universes by broadening the concept of "elsewhere." These universes are located elsewhere, not in ordinary space but in an abstract realm of all possible states. Every conceivable way that the world could be (within the scope of quantum mechanics) corresponds to a different universe. The parallel universes make their presence felt in laboratory experiments, such as wave interference and quantum computation.

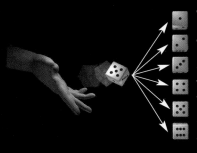

Quantum Dice

Imagine an ideal die whose randomness is purely quantum. When you roll it, the die appears to land on a certain value at random. Quantum mechanics, however, predicts that it lands on all values at once. One way to reconcile these contradictory views is to conclude that the die lands on different values in different universes. In one sixth of the universes, it lands on 1; in one sixth, on 2, and so on. Trapped within one universe, we can perceive only a fraction of the full quantum reality.

Ergodicity

According to the principle of ergodicity, quantum parallel universes are equivalent to more prosaic types of parallel universes. A quantum universe splits over time into multiple universes (*left*). Yet those new universes are no different from parallel universes that already exist somewhere else in space—in, for example, other Level I universes (*right*). The key idea is that parallel universes, of whatever type, embody different ways that events could have unfolded.

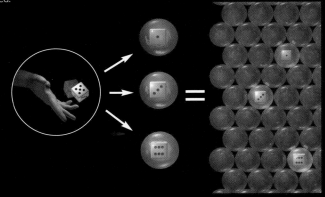

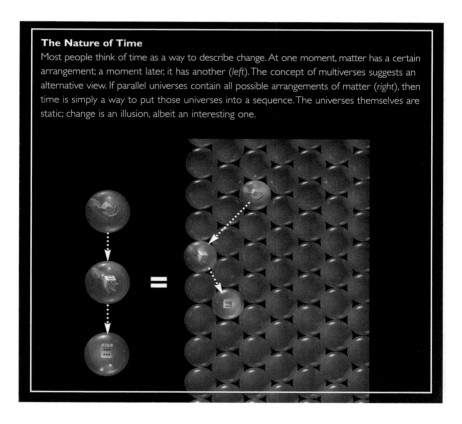

The Nature of Time

Most people think of time as a way to describe change. At one moment, matter has a certain arrangement; a moment later, it has another (*left*). The concept of multiverses suggests an alternative view. If parallel universes contain all possible arrangements of matter (*right*), then time is simply a way to put those universes into a sequence. The universes themselves are static; change is an illusion, albeit an interesting one.

evolves in a deterministic way. There is nothing random or uncertain about it.

The sticky part is how to connect this wave function with what we observe. Many legitimate wave functions correspond to counterintuitive situations, such as a cat being dead and alive at the same time in a so-called superposition. In the 1920s physicists explained away this weirdness by postulating that the wave function "collapsed" into some definite classical outcome whenever someone made an observation. This add-on had the virtue of explaining observations, but it turned an elegant, unitary theory into a kludgy, nonunitary one. The intrinsic randomness commonly ascribed to quantum mechanics is the result of this postulate.

Over the years many physicists have abandoned this view in favor of one developed in 1957 by Princeton graduate student Hugh Everett III. He showed that the collapse postulate is unnecessary. Unadulterated quantum theory does not, in fact, pose any contradictions. Although it predicts that one classical reality gradually splits into superpositions of many such realities, observers subjectively experience this splitting merely as a slight randomness, with probabilities in exact agreement with those from the old collapse postulate. This superposition of classical worlds is the Level III multiverse.

Everett's many-worlds interpretation has been boggling minds inside and outside physics for more than four decades. But the theory becomes easier to grasp when one distinguishes between two ways of viewing a physical theory: the outside view of a physicist studying its mathematical equations, like a bird surveying a landscape from high above it, and the inside view of an observer living in the world described by the equations, like a frog living in the landscape surveyed by the bird.

From the bird perspective, the Level III multiverse is simple. There is only one wave function. It evolves smoothly and deterministically over time without any kind of splitting or parallelism. The abstract quantum world described by this evolving wave function contains within it a vast number of parallel classical story lines, continuously splitting and merging, as well as a number of quantum phenomena that lack a classical description. From their frog perspective, observers perceive only a tiny fraction of this full reality. They can view their own Level I universe, but a process called decoherence—which mimics wave function collapse while preserving unitarity—prevents them from seeing Level III parallel copies of themselves.

Whenever observers are asked a question, make a snap decision and give an answer, quantum effects in their brains lead to a superposition of outcomes, such as "Continue reading the article" and "Put down the article." From the bird perspective, the act of making a decision causes a person to split into multiple copies: one who keeps on reading and one who doesn't. From their frog perspective, however, each of these alter egos is unaware of the others and notices the branching merely as a slight randomness: a certain probability of continuing to read or not.

As strange as this may sound, the exact same situation occurs even in the Level I multiverse. You have evidently decided to keep on reading the article, but one of your alter egos in a distant galaxy put down the magazine after the first paragraph. The only difference between Level I and Level III is where your doppel-gängers reside. In Level I they live elsewhere in good old three-dimensional space. In Level III they live on another quantum branch in infinite-dimensional Hilbert space.

The existence of Level III depends on one crucial assumption: that the time evolution of the wave function is unitary. So far experimenters have encountered no departures from unitarity. In the past few decades they have confirmed unitarity for ever larger systems, including carbon 60 buckyball molecules and kilometer-long optical fibers. On the theoretical side, the case for unitarity has been bolstered by the discovery of decoherence [see "100 Years of Quantum Mysteries," by Max Tegmark and John Archibald Wheeler; *Scientific American*, February 2001]. Some theorists who work on quantum gravity have questioned unitarity; one concern is that evaporating black holes might destroy information, which would be a nonunitary process. But a recent breakthrough in string theory known as AdS/CFT correspondence suggests that even quantum gravity is unitary. If so, black holes do not destroy information but merely transmit it elsewhere.

If physics is unitary, then the standard picture of how quantum fluctuations operated early in the big bang must change. These fluctuations did not generate initial conditions at random. Rather they generated a quantum superposition of all possible initial conditions, which coexisted simultaneously. Decoherence then caused these initial conditions to behave classically in separate quantum branches. Here is the crucial point: the distribution of outcomes on different quantum branches in a given Hubble volume (Level III) is identical to the distribution of outcomes in different Hubble volumes within a single quantum branch (Level I). This property of the quantum fluctuations is known in statistical mechanics as ergodicity.

The same reasoning applies to Level II. The process of symmetry breaking did not produce a unique outcome but rather a superposition of all outcomes, which rapidly went their separate ways. So if physical constants, space-time dimensionality and so on can vary among parallel quantum branches at Level III, then they will also vary among parallel universes at Level II.

In other words, the Level III multiverse adds nothing new beyond Level I and Level II, just more indistinguishable copies of the same universes—the same old story lines playing out again and again in other quantum branches. The passionate debate about Everett's theory therefore seems to be ending in a grand anticlimax, with the discovery of less controversial multiverses (Levels I and II) that are equally large.

Needless to say, the implications are profound, and physicists are only beginning to explore them. For instance, consider the ramifications of the answer to a long-standing question: Does the number of universes exponentially increase over time? The surprising answer is no. From the bird perspective, there is of course only one quantum universe. From the frog perspective, what matters is the number of universes that are distinguishable at a given instant—that is, the number of noticeably different Hubble volumes. Imagine moving planets to random new locations, imagine having married someone

The Mystery of Probability: What Are the Odds?

As multiverse theories gain credence, the sticky issue of how to compute probabilities in physics is growing from a minor nuisance into a major embarrassment. If there are indeed many identical copies of you, the traditional notion of determinism evaporates. You could not compute your own future even if you had complete knowledge of the entire state of the multiverse, because there is no way for you to determine which of these copies is you (they all feel they are). All you can predict, therefore, are probabilities for what you would observe. If an outcome has a probability of, say, 50 percent, it means that half the observers observe that outcome.

Unfortunately, it is not an easy task to compute what fraction of the infinitely many observers perceive what. The answer depends on the order in which you count them. By analogy, the fraction of the integers that are even is 50 percent if you order them numerically (1, 2, 3, 4, . . .) but approaches 100 percent if you sort them digit by digit, the way your word processor would (1, 10, 100, 1,000, . . .). When observers reside in disconnected universes, there is no obviously natural way in which to order them. Instead one must sample from the different universes with some statistical weights referred to by mathematicians as a "measure."

This problem crops up in a mild and treatable manner at Level I, becomes severe at Level II, has caused much debate at Level III, and is horrendous at Level IV. At Level II, for instance, Alexander Vilenkin of Tufts University and others have published predictions for the probability distributions of various cosmological parameters. They have argued that different parallel universes that have inflated by different amounts should be given statistical weights proportional to their volume. On the other hand, any mathematician will tell you that $2 \times 1 = 1$, so there is no objective sense in which an infinite universe that has expanded by a factor of two has gotten larger. Moreover, a finite universe with the topology of a torus is equivalent to a perfectly periodic universe with infinite volume, both from the mathematical bird perspective and from the frog perspective of an observer within it. So why should its infinitely smaller volume give it zero statistical weight? After all, even in the Level I multiverse, Hubble volumes start repeating (albeit in a random order, not periodically) after about 10 to the 10^{118} meters.

If you think that is bad, consider the problem of assigning statistical weights to different mathematical structures at Level IV. The fact that our universe seems relatively simple has led many people to suggest that the correct measure somehow involves complexity. —M. T else, and so on. At the quantum level, there are 10 to the 10^{118} universes with temperatures below 10^8 kelvins. That is a vast number, but a finite one.

From the frog perspective, the evolution of the wave function corresponds to a never-ending sliding from one of these 10 to the 10^{118} states to another. Now you are in universe A, the one in which you are reading this sentence. Now you are in universe B, the one in which you are reading this other sentence. Put differently, universe B has an observer identical to one in universe A, except with an extra instant of memories. All possible states exist at every instant, so the passage of time may be in the eye of the beholder—an idea explored in Greg Egan's 1994 science-fiction novel *Permutation City* and developed by physicist David Deutsch of the University of Oxford, independent physicist Julian Barbour, and others. The multiverse framework may thus prove essential to understanding the nature of time.

Level IV: Other Mathematical Structures

The initial conditions and physical constants in the Level I, Level II and Level III multiverses can vary, but the fundamental laws that govern nature remain the same. Why stop there? Why not allow the laws themselves to vary? How about a universe that obeys the laws of classical physics, with no quantum effects? How about time that comes in discrete steps, as for computers, instead of being continuous? How about a universe that is simply an empty dodecahedron? In the Level IV multiverse, all these alternative realities actually exist.

A hint that such a multiverse might not be just some beer-fueled speculation is the tight correspondence between the worlds of abstract reasoning and of observed reality. Equations and, more generally, mathematical structures such as numbers, vectors and geometric objects describe the world with remarkable verisimilitude. In a famous 1959 lecture, physicist Eugene P. Wigner argued that "the enormous usefulness of mathematics in the natural sciences is something bordering on the mysterious." Conversely, mathematical structures have an eerily real feel to them. They satisfy a central criterion of objective existence: they are the same no matter who studies them. A theorem is true regardless of whether it is proved by a human, a computer or an intelligent dolphin. Contemplative alien civilizations would find the same mathematical structures as we have. Accordingly, mathematicians commonly say that they discover mathematical structures rather than create them.

There are two tenable but diametrically opposed paradigms for understanding the correspondence between mathematics and physics, a dichotomy that arguably goes as far back as Plato and Aristotle. According to the Aristotelian paradigm, physical reality is fundamental and mathematical language is merely a useful approximation. According to the Platonic paradigm, the mathematical

Level IV Multiverse

The ultimate type of parallel universe opens up the full realm of possibility. Universes can differ not just in location, cosmological properties or quantum state but also in the laws of physics. Existing outside of space and time, they are almost impossible to visualize; the best one can do is to think of them abstractly, as static sculptures that represent the mathematical structure of the physical laws that govern them. For example, consider a simple universe: Earth, moon and sun, obeying Newton's laws. To an objective observer, this universe looks like a circular ring (Earth's orbit smeared out in time) wrapped in a braid (the moon's orbit around Earth). Other shapes embody other laws of physics (a, b, c, d). This paradigm solves various problems concerning the foundations of physics.

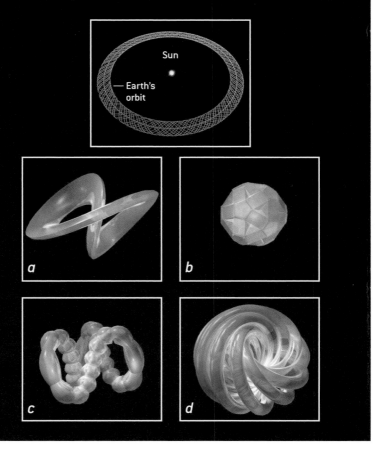

structure is the true reality and observers perceive it imperfectly. In other words, the two paradigms disagree on which is more basic, the frog perspective of the observer or the bird perspective of the physical laws. The Aristotelian paradigm prefers the frog perspective, whereas the Platonic paradigm prefers the bird perspective.

As children, long before we had even heard of mathematics, we were all indoctrinated with the Aristotelian paradigm. The Platonic view is an acquired taste. Modern theoretical physicists tend to be Platonists, suspecting that mathematics describes the universe so well because the universe is inherently mathematical. Then all of physics is ultimately a mathematics problem: a mathematician with unlimited intelligence and resources could in principle compute the frog perspective—that is, compute what self-aware observers the universe contains, what they perceive, and what languages they invent to describe their perceptions to one another.

A mathematical structure is an abstract, immutable entity existing outside of space and time. If history were a movie, the structure would correspond not to a single frame of it but to the entire videotape. Consider, for example, a world made up of pointlike particles moving around in three-dimensional space. In four-dimensional spacetime—the bird perspective—these particle trajectories resemble a tangle of spaghetti. If the frog sees a particle moving with constant velocity, the bird sees a straight strand of uncooked spaghetti. If the frog sees a pair of orbiting particles, the bird sees two spaghetti strands intertwined like a double helix. To the frog, the world is described by Newton's laws of motion and gravitation. To the bird, it is described by the geometry of the pasta—a mathematical structure. The frog itself is merely a thick bundle of pasta, whose highly complex intertwining corresponds to a cluster of particles that store and process information. Our universe is far more complicated than this example, and scientists do not yet know to what, if any, mathematical structure it corresponds.

The Platonic paradigm raises the question of why the universe is the way it is. To an Aristotelian, this is a meaningless question: the universe just is. But a Platonist cannot help but wonder why it could not have been different. If the universe is inherently mathematical, then why was only one of the many mathematical structures singled out to describe a universe? A fundamental asymmetry appears to be built into the very heart of reality.

As a way out of this conundrum, I have suggested that complete mathematical symmetry holds: that all mathematical structures exist physically as well. Every mathematical structure corresponds to a parallel universe. The elements of this multiverse do not reside in the same space but exist outside of space and time. Most of them are probably devoid of observers. This hypothesis can be viewed as a form of radical Platonism, asserting that the mathematical structures in Plato's realm of ideas or the "mindscape" of mathematician

Rudy Rucker of San Jose State University exist in a physical sense. It is akin to what cosmologist John D. Barrow of the University of Cambridge refers to as "π in the sky," what the late Harvard University philosopher Robert Nozick called the principle of fecundity and what the late Princeton philosopher David K. Lewis called modal realism. Level IV brings closure to the hierarchy of multiverses, because any self-consistent fundamental physical theory can be phrased as some kind of mathematical structure.

The Level IV multiverse hypothesis makes testable predictions. As with Level II, it involves an ensemble (in this case, the full range of mathematical structures) and selection effects. As mathematicians continue to categorize mathematical structures, they should find that the structure describing our world is the most generic one consistent with our observations. Similarly, our future observations should be the most generic ones that are consistent with our past observations, and our past observations should be the most generic ones that are consistent with our existence.

Quantifying what "generic" means is a severe problem, and this investigation is only now beginning. But one striking and encouraging feature of mathematical structures is that the symmetry and invariance properties that are responsible for the simplicity and orderliness of our universe tend to be generic, more the rule than the exception. Mathematical structures tend to have them by default, and complicated additional axioms must be added to make them go away.

What Says Occam?

The scientific theories of parallel universes, therefore, form a four-level hierarchy, in which universes become progressively more different from ours. They might have different initial conditions (Level I); different physical constants and particles (Level II); or different physical laws (Level IV). It is ironic that Level III is the one that has drawn the most fire in the past decades, because it is the only one that adds no qualitatively new types of universes.

In the coming decade, dramatically improved cosmo-logical measurements of the microwave background and the large-scale matter distribution will support or refute Level I by further pinning down the curvature and topology of space. These measurements will also probe Level II by testing the theory of chaotic eternal inflation. Progress in both astrophysics and high-energy physics should also clarify the extent to which physical constants are fine-tuned, thereby weakening or strengthening the case for Level II.

If current efforts to build quantum computers succeed, they will provide further evidence for Level III, as they would, in essence, be exploiting the parallelism of the Level III multiverse for parallel computation. Experimenters are also looking for evidence of unitarity violation, which would rule out Level III. Finally, success or failure in the grand challenge of modern physics—unifying general relativity and quantum field theory—will sway opinions on Level IV. Either we will find a mathematical structure that exactly matches our universe, or we will bump up against a limit to the unreasonable effectiveness of mathematics and have to abandon that level.

So should you believe in parallel universes? The principal arguments against them are that they are wasteful and that they are weird. The first argument is that multiverse theories are vulnerable to Occam's razor because they postulate the existence of other worlds that we can never observe. Why should nature be so wasteful and indulge in such opulence as an infinity of different worlds? Yet this argument can be turned around to argue *for* a multiverse. What precisely would nature be wasting? Certainly not space, mass or atoms—the uncontroversial Level I multiverse already contains an infinite amount of all three, so who cares if nature wastes some more? The real issue here is the apparent reduction in simplicity. A skeptic worries about all the information necessary to specify all those unseen worlds.

But an entire ensemble is often much simpler than one of its members. This principle can be stated more formally using the notion of algorithmic information content. The algorithmic information content in a number is, roughly speaking, the length of the shortest computer program that will produce that number as output. For example, consider the set of all integers. Which is simpler, the whole set or just one number? Naively, you might think that a single number is simpler, but the entire set can be generated by quite a trivial computer program, whereas a single number can be hugely long. Therefore, the whole set is actually simpler.

Similarly, the set of all solutions to Einstein's field equations is simpler than a specific solution. The former is described by a few equations, whereas the latter requires the specification of vast amounts of initial data on some hypersurface. The lesson is that complexity increases when we restrict our attention to one particular element in an ensemble, thereby losing the symmetry and simplicity that were inherent in the totality of all the elements taken together.

In this sense, the higher-level multiverses are simpler. Going from our universe to the Level I multiverse eliminates the need to specify initial conditions, upgrading to Level II eliminates the need to specify physical constants, and the Level IV multiverse eliminates the need to specify anything at all. The opulence of complexity is all in the subjective perceptions of observers—the frog perspective. From the bird perspective, the multiverse could hardly be any simpler.

The complaint about weirdness is aesthetic rather than scientific, and it really makes sense only in the Aristotelian worldview. Yet what did we expect? When we ask a profound question about the nature of reality, do we not expect an answer that sounds strange? Evolution provided us with intuition for the everyday physics that had survival value for our distant ancestors, so whenever we venture beyond the everyday world, we should expect it to seem bizarre.

A common feature of all four multiverse levels is that the simplest and arguably most elegant theory involves parallel universes by default. To deny the existence of those universes, one needs to complicate the theory by adding experimentally unsupported processes and ad hoc postulates: finite space, wave function collapse and ontological asymmetry. Our judgment therefore comes down to which we find more wasteful and inelegant: many worlds or many words. Perhaps we will gradually get used to the weird ways of our cosmos and find its strangeness to be part of its charm.

More to Explore

Why Is the CMB Fluctuation Level 10–5? Max Tegmark and Martin Rees in *Astrophysical Journal*, Vol. 499, No. 2, pages 526–532; June 1, 1998. Available online at **arXiv.org/abs/astro-ph/9709058**.

Is "The Theory of Everything" Merely the Ultimate Ensemble Theory? Max Tegmark in *Annals of Physics*, Vol. 270, No.1, pages 1–51; November 20, 1998. Available online at **arXiv.org/abs/gr-qc/9704009**.

Many Worlds in One. Jaume Garriga and Alexander Vilenkin in *Physical Review*, Vol. D64, No. 043511; July 26, 2001. Available online at **arXiv.org/abs/gr-qc/0102010**.

Our Cosmic Habitat. Martin Rees. Princeton University Press, 2001.

Inflation, Quantum Cosmology and the Anthropic
Principle. Andrei Linde in *Science and Ultimate
Reality: From Quantum to Cosmos.* Edited by
J. D. Barrow, P.C.W. Davies and C. L. Harper.
Cambridge University Press, 2003. Available
online at **arXiv.org/abs/hep-th/0211048.**
The author's Web site has more information at
www.hep.upenn.edu/~max/multiverse.html.

About the Author

MAX TEGMARK wrote a four-dimensional version of
the computer game Tetris while in college. In another
universe, he went on to become a highly paid software
developer. In our universe, however, he wound up as
professor of physics and astronomy at the University
of Pennsylvania. Tegmark is an expert in analyzing the
cosmic microwave background and galaxy clustering.
Much of his work bears on the concept of parallel
universes: evaluating evidence for infinite space and
cosmological inflation; developing insights into quantum
decoherence; and studying the possibility that the
amplitude of microwave background fluctuations, the
dimensionality of spacetime and the fundamental laws
of physics can vary from place to place.

"Information in the
4. Holographic Universe"

By Jacob D. Bekenstein

Theoretical results about black holes suggest that the universe could be like a gigantic hologram.

Ask anybody what the physical world is made of, and you are likely to be told "matter and energy." Yet if we have learned anything from engineering, biology and physics, information is just as crucial an ingredient. The robot at the automobile factory is supplied with metal and plastic but can make nothing useful without copious instructions telling it which part to weld to what and so on. A ribosome in a cell in your body is supplied with amino acid building blocks and is powered by energy released by the conversion of ATP to ADP, but it can synthesize no proteins without the information brought to it from the DNA in the cell's nucleus. Likewise, a century of developments in physics has taught us that information is a crucial player in physical systems and processes. Indeed, a current trend, initiated by John A. Wheeler of Princeton University, is to regard the physical world as made of information, with energy and matter as incidentals.

This viewpoint invites a new look at venerable questions. The information storage capacity of devices such as hard disk drives has been increasing by leaps and bounds. When will such progress halt? What is the ultimate information capacity of a device that weighs, say, less than a gram and can fit inside a cubic centimeter (roughly the size of a computer chip)? How much information does it take to describe a whole universe? Could that description fit in a computer's memory? Could we, as William Blake memorably penned, "see the world in a grain of sand," or is that idea no more than poetic license?

Remarkably, recent developments in theoretical physics answer some of these questions, and the answers might be important clues to the ultimate theory of reality. By studying the mysterious properties of black holes, physicists have deduced absolute limits on how much information a region of space or a quantity of matter and energy can hold. Related results suggest that our universe, which we perceive to have three spatial dimensions, might instead be "written" on a two-dimensional surface, like a hologram. Our everyday perceptions of the world as three-dimensional would then be either a profound illusion or merely one of two alternative ways of viewing reality. A grain of sand may not encompass our world, but a flat screen might.

A Tale of Two Entropies

Formal information theory originated in seminal 1948 papers by American applied mathematician Claude E. Shannon, who introduced today's most widely used measure of information content: entropy. Entropy had long been a central concept of thermodynamics, the branch of physics dealing with heat. Thermodynamic entropy is popularly described as the disorder in a physical system. In 1877 Austrian physicist Ludwig Boltzmann characterized it more precisely in terms of the number of distinct microscopic states that the particles composing a chunk of matter could be in while still looking like the same macroscopic chunk of matter. For example, for the air in the room around you, one would count all the ways that the individual gas molecules could be distributed in the room and all the ways they could be moving.

When Shannon cast about for a way to quantify the information contained in, say, a message, he was led by logic to a formula with the same form as Boltzmann's. The Shannon entropy of a message is the number of binary digits, or bits, needed to encode it. Shannon's entropy does not enlighten us about the

---

Overview: The World as a Hologram

- An astonishing theory called the holographic principle holds that the universe is like a hologram: just as a trick of light allows a fully three-dimensional image to be recorded on a flat piece of film, our seemingly three-dimensional universe could be completely equivalent to alternative quantum fields and physical laws "painted" on a distant, vast surface.
- The physics of black holes—immensely dense concentrations of mass—provides a hint that the principle might be true. Studies of black holes show that, although it defies common sense, the maximum entropy or information content of any region of space is defined not by its volume but by its surface area.
- Physicists hope that this surprising finding is a clue to the ultimate theory of reality.

value of information, which is highly dependent on context. Yet as an objective measure of quantity of information, it has been enormously useful in science and technology. For instance, the design of every modern communications device—from cellular phones to modems to compact-disc players—relies on Shannon entropy.

Thermodynamic entropy and Shannon entropy are conceptually equivalent: the number of arrangements that are counted by Boltzmann entropy reflects the amount of Shannon information one would need to implement any particular arrangement. The two entropies have two salient differences, though. First, the thermodynamic entropy used by a chemist or a refrigeration engineer is expressed in units of energy divided by temperature, whereas the Shannon entropy used by a communications engineer is in bits, essentially dimensionless. That difference is merely a matter of convention.

Even when reduced to common units, however, typical values of the two entropies differ vastly in magnitude. A silicon microchip carrying a gigabyte of data, for instance, has a Shannon entropy of about 10^{10} bits (one byte is eight bits), tremendously smaller than the chip's thermodynamic entropy, which is about 10^{23} bits at room temperature. This discrepancy occurs because the entropies are computed for different degrees of freedom. A degree of freedom is any quantity that can vary, such as a coordinate specifying a particle's location or one component of its velocity. The Shannon entropy of the chip cares only about the overall state of each tiny transistor etched in the silicon crystal—the transistor is on or off; it is a 0 or a 1—a single binary degree of freedom. Thermodynamic entropy, in contrast, depends on the states of all the billions of atoms (and their roaming electrons) that make up each transistor. As miniaturization brings closer the day when each atom will store one bit of information for us, the useful Shannon entropy of the state-of-the-art microchip will edge closer in magnitude to its material's thermodynamic entropy. When the two entropies are calculated for the same degrees of freedom, they are equal.

What are the ultimate degrees of freedom? Atoms, after all, are made of electrons and nuclei, nuclei are agglomerations of protons and neutrons, and those in turn are composed of quarks. Many physicists today consider electrons and quarks to be excitations of superstrings, which they hypothesize to be the most fundamental entities. But the vicissitudes of a century of revelations in physics warn us not to be dogmatic. There could be more levels of structure in our universe than are dreamt of in today's physics.

One cannot calculate the ultimate information capacity of a chunk of matter or, equivalently, its true thermodynamic entropy, without knowing the nature of the ultimate constituents of matter or of the deepest level of structure, which I shall refer to as level X. (This ambiguity causes no problems in analyzing practical

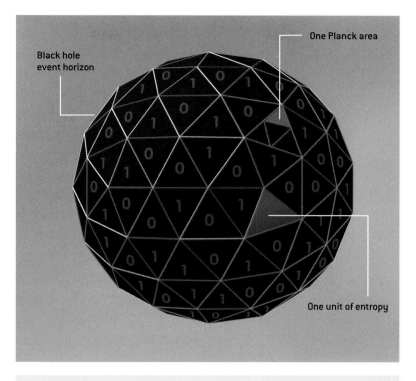

The entropy of a black hole is proportional to the area of its event horizon, the surface within which even light cannot escape the gravity of the hole. Specifically, a hole with a horizon spanning A Planck areas has $A/4$ units of entropy. (The Planck area, approximately 10^{-66} square centimeter, is the fundamental quantum unit of area determined by the strength of gravity, the speed of light and the size of quanta.) Considered as information, it is as if the entropy were written on the event horizon, with each bit (each digital 1 or 0) corresponding to four Planck areas.

thermodynamics, such as that of car engines, for example, because the quarks within the atoms can be ignored—they do not change their states under the relatively benign conditions in the engine.) Given the dizzying progress in miniaturization, one can playfully contemplate a day when quarks will serve to store information, one bit apiece perhaps. How much information would then fit into our one-centimeter cube? And how much if we harness superstrings or even deeper, yet undreamt of levels? Surprisingly, developments in gravitation physics in the past three decades have supplied some clear answers to what seem to be elusive questions.

Black Hole Thermodynamics

A central player in these developments is the black hole. Black holes are a consequence of general relativity, Albert Einstein's 1915 geometric theory of gravitation. In this theory, gravitation arises from the curvature of spacetime, which makes objects move as if they were pulled by a force. Conversely, the curvature is caused by the presence of matter and energy. According to Einstein's equations, a sufficiently dense concentration of matter or energy will curve spacetime so extremely that it rends, forming a black hole. The laws of relativity forbid anything that went into a black hole from coming out again, at least within the classical (nonquantum) description of the physics. The point of no return, called the event horizon of the black hole, is of crucial importance. In the simplest case, the horizon is a sphere, whose surface area is larger for more massive black holes.

It is impossible to determine what is inside a black hole. No detailed information can emerge across the horizon and escape into the outside world. In disappearing forever into a black hole, however, a piece of matter does leave some traces. Its energy (we count any mass as energy in accordance with Einstein's $E = mc^2$) is permanently reflected in an increment in the black hole's mass. If the matter is captured while circling the hole, its associated angular momentum is added to the black hole's angular momentum. Both the mass and angular momentum of a black hole are measurable from their effects on spacetime around the hole. In this way, the laws of conservation of energy and angular momentum are upheld by black holes. Another fundamental law, the second law of thermodynamics, appears to be violated.

The second law of thermodynamics summarizes the familiar observation that most processes in nature are irreversible: a teacup falls from the table and shatters, but no one has ever seen shards jump up of their own accord and assemble into a teacup. The second law of thermodynamics forbids such inverse processes. It states that the entropy of an isolated physical system can never decrease; at best, entropy remains constant, and usually it increases. This law is central to physical chemistry and engineering; it is arguably the physical law with the greatest impact outside physics.

As first emphasized by Wheeler, when matter disappears into a black hole, its entropy is gone for good, and the second law seems to be transcended, made irrelevant. A clue to resolving this puzzle came in 1970, when Demetrious Christodoulou, then a graduate student of Wheeler's at Princeton, and Stephen W. Hawking of the University of Cambridge independently proved that in various processes, such as black hole mergers, the total area of the event horizons never decreases. The analogy with the tendency of entropy to increase led me to propose in 1972 that a black hole has entropy proportional to the area of its horizon [see "The Entropy of a Black Hole" box]. I conjectured that when matter falls into a black hole, the increase in black hole entropy always compensates or overcompensates for the "lost" entropy of the matter. More generally, the sum of black hole entropies and the ordinary entropy outside the black holes cannot decrease. This is the generalized second law— GSL for short.

The GSL has passed a large number of stringent, if purely theoretical, tests. When a star collapses to form a black hole, the black hole entropy greatly exceeds the star's entropy. In 1974 Hawking demonstrated that a black hole spontaneously emits thermal radiation, now known as Hawking radiation, by a quantum process [see "The Quantum Mechanics of Black Holes," by Stephen W. Hawking; *Scientific American*, January 1977]. The Christodoulou-Hawking theorem fails in the face of this phenomenon (the mass of the black hole, and therefore its horizon area, decreases), but the GSL copes with it: the entropy of the emergent radiation more than compensates for the decrement in black hole entropy, so the GSL is preserved. In 1986 Rafael D. Sorkin of Syracuse University exploited the horizon's role in barring information inside the black hole from influencing affairs outside to show that the GSL (or something very similar to it) must be valid for any conceivable process that black holes undergo. His deep argument makes it clear that the entropy entering the GSL is that calculated down to level X, whatever that level may be.

Hawking's radiation process allowed him to determine the proportionality constant between black hole entropy and horizon area: black hole entropy is precisely one quarter of the event horizon's area measured in Planck areas. (The Planck length, about 10^{-33} centimeter, is the fundamental length scale related to gravity and quantum mechanics. The Planck area is its square.) Even in thermodynamic terms, this is a vast quantity of entropy. The entropy of a black hole one centimeter in diameter would be about 10^{66} bits, roughly equal to the thermodynamic entropy of a cube of water 10 billion kilometers on a side.

The World as a Hologram

The GSL allows us to set bounds on the information capacity of any isolated physical system, limits that refer to the information at all levels of structure down to level X. In 1980 I began studying the first such bound, called the universal entropy bound, which

Limits on Information Density

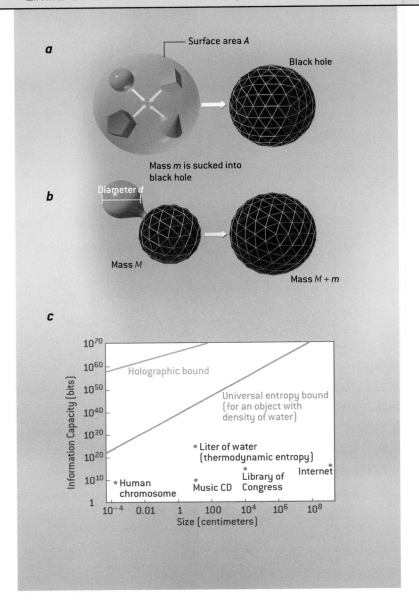

a Surface area *A*

Black hole

Mass *m* is sucked into black hole

b Diameter *d*

Mass *M*

Mass *M + m*

c

Information Capacity (bits)

Holographic bound

Universal entropy bound (for an object with density of water)

• Liter of water (thermodynamic entropy)

• Human chromosome

• Music CD

• Library of Congress

• Internet

Size (centimeters)

The thermodynamics of black holes allows one to deduce limits on the density of entropy or information in various circumstances.

The holographic bound defines how much information can be contained in a specified region of space. It can be derived by considering a roughly spherical distribution of matter that is contained within a surface of area A. The matter is induced to collapse to form a black hole (a). The black hole's area must be smaller than A, so its entropy must be less than $A/4$. Because entropy cannot decrease, one infers that the original distribution of matter also must carry less than $A/4$ units of entropy or information. This result—that the maximum information content of a region of space is fixed by its area—defies the commonsense expectation that the capacity of a region should depend on its volume.

The universal entropy bound defines how much information can be carried by a mass m of diameter d. It is derived by imagining that a capsule of matter is engulfed by a black hole not much wider than it (b). The increase in the black hole's size places a limit on how much entropy the capsule could have contained. This limit is tighter than the holographic bound, except when the capsule is almost as dense as a black hole (in which case the two bounds are equivalent).

The holographic and universal information bounds are far beyond the data storage capacities of any current technology, and they greatly exceed the density of information on chromosomes and the thermodynamic entropy of water (c).

—J. D. B.

limits how much entropy can be carried by a specified mass of a specified size [see "Limits on Information Density" box]. A related idea, the holographic bound, was devised in 1995 by Leonard Susskind of Stanford University. It limits how much entropy can be contained in matter and energy occupying a specified volume of space.

In his work on the holographic bound, Susskind considered any approximately spherical isolated mass that is not itself a black hole and that fits inside a closed

The information content of a pile of computer chips increases in proportion with the number of chips or, equivalently, the volume they occupy. That simple rule must break down for a large enough pile of chips because eventually the information would exceed the holographic bound, which depends on the surface area, not the volume. The "breakdown" occurs when the immense pile of chips collapses to form a black hole.

surface of area A. If the mass can collapse to a black hole, that hole will end up with a horizon area smaller than A. The black hole entropy is therefore smaller than $A/4$. According to the GSL, the entropy of the system cannot decrease, so the mass's original entropy cannot have been bigger than $A/4$. It follows that the entropy of an isolated physical system with boundary area A is necessarily less than $A/4$. What if the mass does not spontaneously collapse? In 2000 I showed that a tiny black hole can be used to convert the system to a black hole not much different from the one in Susskind's argument. The bound is therefore independent of the constitution of the system or of the nature of level X. It just depends on the GSL.

We can now answer some of those elusive questions about the ultimate limits of information storage. A device measuring a centimeter across could in principle hold up to 10^{66} bits—a mind-boggling amount. The visible universe contains at least 10^{100} bits of entropy, which could in principle be packed inside a sphere a tenth of a light-year across. Estimating the entropy of the universe is a difficult problem, however, and much larger numbers, requiring a sphere almost as big as the universe itself, are entirely plausible.

But it is another aspect of the holographic bound that is truly astonishing. Namely, that the maximum possible entropy depends on the boundary area instead of the volume. Imagine that we are piling up computer memory chips in a big heap. The number of transistors— the total data storage capacity—increases with the volume of the heap. So, too, does the total thermodynamic entropy of all the chips. Remarkably, though, the theoretical ultimate information capacity of the space occupied by the heap increases only with the surface area. Because volume increases more rapidly than surface area, at some point the entropy of all the chips would exceed the holographic bound. It would seem that either the GSL or our commonsense ideas of entropy and information capacity must fail. In fact, what fails is the pile itself: it would collapse under its own gravity and form a black hole before that impasse was reached. Thereafter each additional memory chip would increase the mass and surface area of the black hole in a way that would continue to preserve the GSL.

This surprising result—that information capacity depends on surface area—has a natural explanation if the holographic *principle* (proposed in 1993 by Nobelist Gerard 't Hooft of the University of Utrecht in the Netherlands and elaborated by Susskind) is true. In the everyday world, a hologram is a special kind of photograph that generates a full three-dimensional image when it is illuminated in the right manner. All the information describing the 3-D scene is encoded into the pattern of light and dark areas on the two-dimensional piece of film, ready to be regenerated. The holographic principle contends that an analogue of this visual magic applies to the full physical description of any system occupying a 3-D region: it proposes that another physical theory defined only on the 2-D boundary of the region completely describes the 3-D physics. If a 3-D system can be fully described by a physical theory operating solely on its 2-D boundary, one would expect the information content of the system not to exceed that of the description on the boundary.

A Universe Painted on Its Boundary

Can we apply the holographic principle to the universe at large? The real universe is a 4-D system: it has volume and extends in time. If the physics of our universe is

A Holographic Spacetime

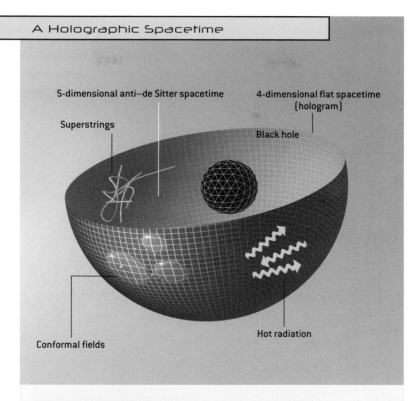

5-dimensional anti–de Sitter spacetime

Superstrings

4-dimensional flat spacetime (hologram)

Black hole

Conformal fields

Hot radiation

Two universes of different dimension and obeying disparate physical laws are rendered completely equivalent by the holographic principle. Theorists have demonstrated this principle mathematically for a specific type of five-dimensional spacetime ("anti–de Sitter") and its four-dimensional boundary. In effect, the 5-D universe is recorded like a hologram on the 4-D surface at its periphery. Superstring theory rules in the 5-D spacetime, but a so-called conformal field theory of point particles operates on the 4-D hologram. A black hole in the 5-D spacetime is equivalent to hot radiation on the hologram—for example, the hole and the radiation have the same entropy even though the physical origin of the entropy is completely different for each case. Although these two descriptions of the universe seem utterly unlike, no experiment could distinguish between them, even in principle. —J. D. B.

holographic, there would be an alternative set of physical laws, operating on a 3-D boundary of spacetime somewhere, that would be equivalent to our known 4-D physics. We do not yet know of any such 3-D theory that works in that way. Indeed, what surface should we use as the boundary of the universe? One step toward realizing these ideas is to study models that are simpler than our real universe.

A class of concrete examples of the holographic principle at work involves so-called anti–de Sitter spacetimes. The original de Sitter spacetime is a model universe first obtained by Dutch astronomer Willem de Sitter in 1917 as a solution of Einstein's equations, including the repulsive force known as the cosmological constant. De Sitter's spacetime is empty, expands at an accelerating rate and is very highly symmetrical. In 1997 astronomers studying distant supernova explosions concluded that our universe now expands in an accelerated fashion and will probably become increasingly like a de Sitter spacetime in the future. Now, if the repulsion in Einstein's equations is changed to attraction, de Sitter's solution turns into the anti–de Sitter spacetime, which has equally as much symmetry. More important for the holographic concept, it possesses a boundary, which is located "at infinity" and is a lot like our everyday spacetime.

Using anti–de Sitter spacetime, theorists have devised a concrete example of the holographic principle at work: a universe described by superstring theory functioning in an anti–de Sitter spacetime is completely equivalent to a quantum field theory operating on the boundary of that spacetime [see "A Holographic Spacetime" box]. Thus, the full majesty of superstring theory in an anti–de Sitter universe is painted on the boundary of the universe. Juan Maldacena, then at Harvard University, first conjectured such a relation in 1997 for the 5-D anti–de Sitter case, and it was later confirmed for many situations by Edward Witten of the Institute for Advanced Study in Princeton, N.J., and Steven S. Gubser, Igor R. Klebanov and Alexander M. Polyakov of Princeton University. Examples of this holographic correspondence are now known for spacetimes with a variety of dimensions.

This result means that two ostensibly very different theories—not even acting in spaces of the same dimension—are equivalent. Creatures living in one of these universes would be incapable of determining if they inhabited a 5-D universe described by string theory or a 4-D one described by a quantum field theory of point particles. (Of course, the structures of their brains might give them an overwhelming "commonsense" prejudice in favor of one description or another, in just the way that our brains construct an innate perception that our universe has three spatial dimensions.)

The holographic equivalence can allow a difficult calculation in the 4-D boundary spacetime, such as the behavior of quarks and gluons, to be traded for another, easier calculation in the highly symmetric, 5-D anti–de Sitter spacetime. The correspondence works the other way, too. Witten has shown that a black hole in anti–de

Sitter spacetime corresponds to hot radiation in the alternative physics operating on the bounding spacetime. The entropy of the hole—a deeply mysterious concept— equals the radiation's entropy, which is quite mundane.

The Expanding Universe

Highly symmetric and empty, the 5-D anti–de Sitter universe is hardly like our universe existing in 4-D, filled with matter and radiation, and riddled with violent events. Even if we approximate our real universe with one that has matter and radiation spread uniformly throughout, we get not an anti–de Sitter universe but rather a "Friedmann-Robertson-Walker" universe. Most cosmologists today concur that our universe resembles an FRW universe, one that is infinite, has no boundary and will go on expanding ad infinitum.

Does such a universe conform to the holographic principle or the holographic bound? Susskind's argument based on collapse to a black hole is of no help here. Indeed, the holographic bound deduced from black holes must break down in a uniform expanding universe. The entropy of a region uniformly filled with matter and radiation is truly proportional to its volume. A sufficiently large region will therefore violate the holographic bound.

In 1999 Raphael Bousso, then at Stanford, proposed a modified holographic bound, which has since been found to work even in situations where the bounds we discussed earlier cannot be applied. Bousso's formulation starts with any suitable 2-D surface; it may be closed like a sphere or open like a sheet of paper. One then imagines a brief burst of light issuing simultaneously and perpendicularly from all over one side of the surface. The only demand is that the imaginary light rays are converging to start with. Light emitted from the inner surface of a spherical shell, for instance, satisfies that requirement. One then considers the entropy of the matter and radiation that these imaginary rays traverse, up to the points where they start crossing. Bousso conjectured that this entropy cannot exceed the entropy represented by the initial surface—one quarter of its area, measured in Planck areas. This is a different way of tallying up the entropy than that used in the original holographic bound. Bousso's bound refers not to the entropy of a region at one time but rather to the sum of entropies of locales at a variety of times: those that are "illuminated" by the light burst from the surface.

Bousso's bound subsumes other entropy bounds while avoiding their limitations. Both the universal entropy bound and the 't Hooft-Susskind form of the holographic bound can be deduced from Bousso's for any isolated system that is not evolving rapidly and whose gravitational field is not strong. When these conditions are overstepped—as for a collapsing sphere of matter already inside a black hole—these bounds eventually fail, whereas Bousso's bound continues to hold. Bousso has also shown that his strategy can be

Our innate perception that the world is three-dimensional could be an extraordinary illusion.

used to locate the 2-D surfaces on which holograms of the world can be set up.

Augurs of a Revolution

Researchers have proposed many other entropy bounds. The proliferation of variations on the holographic motif makes it clear that the subject has not yet reached the status of physical law. But although the holographic way of thinking is not yet fully understood, it seems to be here to stay. And with it comes a realization that the fundamental belief, prevalent for 50 years, that field theory is the ultimate language of physics must give way. Fields, such as the electromagnetic field, vary continuously from point to point, and they thereby describe an infinity of degrees of freedom. Superstring theory also embraces an infinite number of degrees of freedom. Holography restricts the number of degrees of freedom that can be present inside a bounding surface to a finite number; field theory with its infinity cannot be the final story. Furthermore, even if the infinity is tamed, the mysterious dependence of information on surface area must be somehow accommodated.

Holography may be a guide to a better theory. What is the fundamental theory like? The chain of reasoning involving holography suggests to some, notably Lee Smolin of the Perimeter Institute for Theoretical Physics in Waterloo, that such a final theory must be concerned not with fields, not even with spacetime, but rather with information exchange among physical processes. If so, the vision of information as the stuff the world is made of will have found a worthy embodiment.

More to Explore

Black Hole Thermodynamics. Jacob D. Bekenstein in *Physics Today*, Vol. 33, No. 1, pages 24–31; January 1980.
Black Holes and Time Warps: Einstein's Outrageous Legacy. Kip S. Thorne. W. W. Norton, 1995.

Black Holes and the Information Paradox. Leonard Susskind in *Scientific American*, Vol. 276, No. 4, pages 52–57; April 1997.
The Universe in a Nutshell. Stephen Hawking. Bantam Books, 2001.
Three Roads to Quantum Gravity. Lee Smolin. Basic Books, 2002.

About the Author

JACOB D. BEKENSTEIN has contributed to the foundation of black hole thermodynamics and to other aspects of the connections between information and gravitation. He is Polak Professor of Theoretical Physics at the Hebrew University of Jerusalem, a member of the Israel Academy of Sciences and Humanities, and a recipient of the Rothschild Prize. Bekenstein dedicates this article to John Archibald Wheeler (his Ph.D. supervisor 30 years ago). Wheeler belongs to the third generation of Ludwig Boltzmann's students: Wheeler's Ph.D. adviser, Karl Herzfeld, was a student of Boltzmann's student Friedrich Hasenöhrl.

"The Future of String Theory: A Conversation with Brian Greene"

By George Musser

String theory used to get everyone all tied up in knots. Even its practitioners fretted about how complicated it was, while other physicists mocked its lack of experimental predictions. The rest of the world was largely oblivious. Scientists could scarcely communicate just why string theory was so exciting—why it could fulfill Albert Einstein's dream of the ultimate unified theory, how it could give insight into such deep questions as why the universe exists at all. But in the mid-1990s the theory started to click together conceptually. It made some testable, if qualified, predictions. The outside world began to pay attention. Woody Allen satirized the theory in a *New Yorker* column this past July— probably the first time anyone has used Calabi-Yau spaces to make a point about interoffice romance.

Few people can take more credit for demystifying string theory than Brian Greene, a Columbia University physics professor and a major contributor to the theory. His 1999 book *The Elegant Universe* reached number four on the *New York Times* best-seller list and was a finalist for the Pulitzer Prize. Greene is now host of a three-part Nova series on PBS and has just completed a book on the nature of space and time. *Scientific American* staff editor George Musser recently spoke with him over a plate of stringy spaghetti. Here is an abridged, edited version of that conversation.

Scientific American: Sometimes when our readers hear the words "string theory" or "cosmology," they throw up their hands and say, "I'll never understand it."

BRIAN GREENE: *I've definitely encountered a certain amount of intimidation at the outset when it comes to ideas like string theory or cosmology. But what I have found is that the basic interest is so widespread and so deep in most people that I've spoken with, that there is a willingness to go a little bit further than you might with other subjects that are more easily taken in.*

SA: I noticed that at several points in *The Elegant Universe*, you first gave a rough idea of the physics concepts and then the detailed version.

BG: *I found that to be a useful way of going about it, especially in the harder parts. It gives the reader permission: If the rough idea is the level at which you want to take it in, that's great; feel free to skip this next stuff. If not, go for it. I like to say things more than one way. I just think that when it comes to abstract ideas, you need many roads into them. From the scientific point of view, if you stick with one road, I think you really compromise your ability*

to make breakthroughs. I think that's really what breakthroughs are about. Everybody's looking at a problem one way, and you come at it from the back. That different way of getting there somehow reveals things that the other approach didn't.

SA: What are some examples of that back-door approach?

BG: *Well, probably the biggest ones are Ed Witten's breakthroughs. Ed [of the Institute for Advanced Study in Princeton, N.J.] just walked up the mountain and looked down and saw the connections that* *nobody else saw and in that way united the five string theories that previously were thought to be completely distinct. It was all out there; he just took a different perspective, and bang, it all came together. And that's genius.*

To me that suggests what a fundamental discovery is. The universe in a sense guides us toward truths, because those truths are the things that govern what we see. If we're all being governed by what we see, we're all being steered in the same direction. Therefore, the difference between making a breakthrough and not often can be just a small element of perception, either true perception or mathematical perception, that puts things together in a different way.

SA: Do you think that these discoveries would have been made without the intervention of genius?

BG: *Well, it's tough to say. In the case of string theory, I think so, because the pieces of the puzzle were really becoming clearer and clearer. It may have been five or 10 years later, but I suspect it would have happened. But with general relativity, I don't know. General relativity is such a leap, such a monumental rethinking of space, time and gravity, that it's not obvious to me how and when that would have happened without Einstein.*

SA: Are there examples in string theory that you think are analogous to that huge leap?

BG: *I think we're still waiting for a leap of that magnitude. String theory has been built up out of a lot of smaller ideas that a lot of people have contributed and been slowly stitching together into an ever more impressive theoretical edifice. But what idea sits at the top of that edifice, we still don't really know. When we do have that idea, I believe that it will be like a beacon shining down; it will illuminate the edifice, and it will also, I believe, give answers to critical questions that remain unresolved.*

SA: In the case of relativity, you had the equivalence principle and general covariance in that beacon role. In the Standard Model, it's gauge invariance. In *The Elegant Universe* you suggested the holographic principle could be that principle for string theory [see also "Information in the Holographic Universe," by Jacob D. Bekenstein; *Scientific American*, August]. What's your thinking on that now?

BG: *Well, the past few years have only seen the holographic principle rise to a yet greater prominence and believability. Back in the mid-'90s, shortly after the holographic ideas were suggested, the supporting ideas were rather abstract and vague, all based upon features of black holes: Black hole entropy resides on the surface; therefore, maybe the degrees of freedom reside on the surface; therefore, maybe that's true of all regions that have a horizon; maybe it's true of cosmological horizons; maybe we're living* *within a cosmological region which has its true degrees of freedom far away. Wonderfully strange ideas, but the supporting evidence was meager.*

But that changed with the work of Juan Maldacena [of the Institute for Advanced Study in Princeton, N.J.], in which he found an explicit example within string theory, where physics in the bulk—that is, in the arena that we consider to be real—would be exactly mirrored by physics taking place on a bounding surface. There'd be no difference in terms of the ability of either description to truly describe what's going on, yet in detail the descriptions would be vastly different. One would be in five dimensions, the other in four. So even the number of dimensions seems not to be something which you can count on, because there can be alternative descriptions that would accurately reflect the physics you're observing.

So to my mind, that makes the abstract ideas now concrete; it makes you believe the abstract ideas. And even if the details of string theory change, I think, as many others do—not everyone, though— that the holographic idea will persist and will guide us. Whether it truly is the idea, I don't know. I don't think so. But I think that it could well be one of the key stepping-stones towards finding the essential ideas of the theory. It steps outside the details of the theory and just says, Here's a very general feature of a world that has quantum mechanics and gravity.

SA: Let's talk a bit about loop quantum gravity and some of the other approaches. You've always described string theory as the only game in town when it comes to quantum gravity. Do you still feel that way?

BG: *Well, I think it's the most fun game in town! But to be fair, the loop-quantum-gravity community has made tremendous progress. There are still many very basic questions that I don't feel have been answered, not to my satisfaction. But it's a viable approach, and it's great there are such large numbers of extremely talented people working on it. My hope—and it has been one that Lee Smolin [of the Perimeter Institute in Waterloo, Canada] has championed—is that ultimately we're developing the same theory from different angles. It's far from impossible that we're going down our route to quantum gravity, they're going down their route to quantum gravity, and we're going to meet someplace. Because it turns out that many of their strengths are our weaknesses. Many of our strengths are their weaknesses.*

One weakness of string theory is that it's so-called background-dependent. We need to assume an existing spacetime within which the strings move. You'd hope, though, that a true quantum theory of gravity would have spacetime emerge from its fundamental equations. They [the loop-quantum gravity researchers], however, do have a background-independent formulation in their approach, where spacetime does emerge more fundamentally from the theory itself. On the other hand, we are able to make very direct contact with Einstein's general relativity on large scales. We see it in our equations. They have some difficulty making contact with ordinary gravity. So naturally, you'd think maybe one could put together the strengths of each.

SA: Has that effort been made?

BG: *Slowly. There are very few people who are really well versed in both theories. These are both two huge subjects, and you can spend your whole life, every moment of your working day, just in your own subject, and you still won't know everything that's going on. But many people are heading down that path and starting to think along those lines, and there have been some joint meetings.*

SA: If you have this background dependence, what hope is there to really understand, in a deep sense, what space and time are?

BG: *Well, you can chip away at the problem. For instance, even with background dependence, we've learned things like mirror symmetry—there can be two spacetimes, one physics. We've learned topology change—that space can evolve in ways that we wouldn't have thought possible before. We've* *learned that the microworld might be governed by noncommutative geometry, where the coordinates, unlike real numbers, depend upon the order in which you multiply them. So you can get hints. You can get isolated glimpses of what's truly going on down there. But I think without the background-independent formalism, it's going to be hard to put the pieces together on their own.*

SA: The mirror symmetry is incredibly profound, because it divorces spacetime geometry from physics. The connection between the two was always the Einsteinian program.

BG: *That's right. Now, it doesn't divorce them completely. It simply says that you're missing half of the story. Geometry is tightly tied to physics, but it's a two-to-one map. It's not physics and geometry. It's physics and geometry-geometry, and which geometry you want to pick is up to you. Sometimes using one geometry gives you more insight than the other. Again, different ways of looking at one and the same physical system: two different geometries and one physics. And people have found there are mathematical questions about certain physical and geometrical systems that people couldn't answer using the one geometry. Bring in the mirror geometry that had previously gone unrealized, and, all of a sudden, profoundly difficult questions, when translated, were mind-bogglingly simple.*

SA: Can you describe noncommutative geometry?

BG: *Since the time of Descartes, we've found it very powerful to label points by their coordinates, either on Earth by their latitude and longitude or in three-space by the three Cartesian coordinates, x, y and z, that you learn in high school. And we've always imagined that those numbers are like ordinary numbers, which have the property that, when you multiply them together—which is often an operation you need to do in physics—the answer doesn't depend on the order of operation: 3 times 5 is 5 times 3. What we seem to be finding is that when you coordinatize space on very small scales, the numbers involved are not like 3's and 5's, which don't depend upon the order in which they're multiplied. There's a new class of numbers that* do *depend on the order of multiplication.*

They're actually not that new, because for a long time we have known of an entity called the matrix. Sure as shooting, matrix multiplication depends upon the order of multiplication. A times B does not equal B times A if A and B are matrices. String theory seems to indicate that points described by single numbers are replaced by geometrical objects described by matrices. On big scales, it turns out that these matrices become more and more diagonal, and diagonal matrices do have the property that they commute when you multiply. It doesn't matter how you multiply A times B if they're diagonal matrices.

But then if you venture into the microworld, the off-diagonal entries in the matrices get bigger and bigger and bigger until way down in the depths, they are playing a significant part.

Noncommutative geometry is a whole new field of geometry that some people have been developing for years without necessarily an application of physics in mind. The French mathematician Alain Connes has this big thick book called Noncommutative Geometry. *Euclid and Gauss and Riemann and all those wonderful geometers were working in the context of commutative geometry, and now Connes and others are taking off and developing the newer structure of noncommutative geometry.*

SA: It is baffling to me—maybe it *should* be baffling—that you would have to label points with a matrix or some nonpure number. What does that mean?

BG: *The way to think about it is: There is no notion of a point. A point is an approximation. If there is a point, you should label it by a number. But the claim is that, on sufficiently small scales, that language of points becomes such a poor approximation that it just isn't relevant. When we talk about points in geometry, we really talk about how something can move through points. It's the motion of objects that ultimately is what's relevant. Their motion, it turns out, can be more complicated than just sliding back and forth. All those motions are captured by a*

If you were a string, spacetime might look something like this: six extra dimensions curled into a so-called Calabi-Yau shape.

matrix. So rather than labeling an object by what point it's passing through, you need to label its motion by this matrix of degrees of freedom.

SA: What is your current thinking on anthropic and multiverse-type ideas? You talked about it in *The Elegant Universe* in the context of whether there is some limit to the explanatory power of string theory.

BG: *I and many others have never been too happy with any of these anthropic ideas, largely because it seems* to me that at any point in the history of science, you can say, "Okay, we're done, we can't go any further, and the final answer to every currently unsolved question is: 'Things are the way they are because had they not been this way, we wouldn't have been here to ask the question.'" So it sort of feels like a cop-out. Maybe that's the wrong word. Not necessarily like a cop-out; it feels a little dangerous to me, because maybe you just needed five more years of hard work and you would have answered those unresolved questions, rather than just chalking them up to, "That's just how it is." So that's my concern: that one doesn't stop looking by virtue of having this fallback position.

But you know, it's definitely the case that the anthropic ideas have become more developed. They're now real proposals whereby you would have many universes, and those many universes could all have different properties, and it very well could be that we're simply in this one because the properties are right for us to be here, and we're not in those others because we couldn't survive there. It's less of just a mental exercise.

SA: String theory, and modern physics generally, seem to be approaching a single logical structure that *had* to be the way it is; the theory is the way it is because there's no other way it could be. On the one hand, that would argue against an anthropic direction. But on the other hand, there's a flexibility in the theory that leads you to an anthropic direction.

BG: The flexibility may or may not truly be there. That really could be an artifact of our lack of full understanding. But were I to go by what we understand today, the theory seems to be able to give rise to many different worlds, of which ours seems to be potentially one, but not even necessarily a very special one. So yes, there is a tension with the goal of absolute, rigid inflexibility.

SA: If you had other grad students waiting in the wings, what would you steer them to?

BG: Well, the big questions are, I think, the ones that we've discussed. Can we understand where space and time come from? Can we figure out the fundamental ideas of string theory or M-theory? Can we show that this fundamental idea yields a unique theory with the unique solution, which happens to be the world as we know it? Is it possible to test these ideas through astronomical observations or through accelerator-based experiment?

Can we even take a step further back and understand why quantum mechanics had to be part and parcel of the world as we know it? How many of the things that we rely on at a very deep level in any physical theory that has a chance of being right—such as space, time, quantum mechanics—are truly essential, and how many of them can be relaxed and potentially still yield the world that appears close to ours?

Could physics have taken a different path that would have been experimentally as successful but completely different? I don't know. But I think it's a real interesting question to ask. How much of what we believe is truly fundamentally driven in a unique way by data and mathematical consistency, and how much of it could have gone one way or another, and we just happened to go down one path because that's what we happened to discover? Could beings on another planet have completely different sets of laws that somehow work just as well as ours?

On the Web

The full transcript of this conversation, with comments on everything from television to the arrow of time, is available at **www.sciam.com.**

6. "Atoms of Space and Time"

By Lee Smolin

We perceive space and time to be continuous, but if the amazing theory of loop quantum gravity is correct, they actually come in discrete pieces.

A little more than 100 years ago most people— and most scientists—thought of matter as continuous. Although since ancient times some philosophers and scientists had speculated that if matter were broken up into small enough bits, it might turn out to be made up of very tiny atoms, few thought the existence of atoms could ever be proved. Today we have imaged individual atoms and have studied the particles that compose them. The granularity of matter is old news.

In recent decades, physicists and mathematicians have asked if space is also made of discrete pieces. Is it continuous, as we learn in school, or is it more like a piece of cloth, woven out of individual fibers? If we could probe to size scales that were small enough, would we see "atoms" of space, irreducible pieces of volume that cannot be broken into anything smaller? And what about time: Does nature change continuously, or does the world evolve in series of very tiny steps, acting more like a digital computer?

The past 16 years have seen great progress on these questions. A theory with the strange name of "loop quantum gravity" predicts that space and time are indeed made of discrete pieces. The picture revealed by calculations carried out within the framework of this theory is both simple and beautiful. The theory has deepened our understanding of puzzling phenomena having to do with black holes and the big bang. Best of all, it is testable; it makes predictions for experiments that can be done in the near future that will enable us to detect the atoms of space, if they are really there.

Quanta

My colleagues and I developed the theory of loop quantum gravity while struggling with a long-standing problem in physics: Is it possible to develop a quantum theory of gravity? To explain why this is an important question—and what it has to do with the granularity of space and time—I must first say a bit about quantum theory and the theory of gravity.

The theory of quantum mechanics was formulated in the first quarter of the 20th century, a development that was closely connected with the confirmation that matter is made of atoms. The equations of quantum mechanics require that certain quantities, such as the energy of an atom, can come only in specific, discrete units. Quantum theory successfully predicts the properties and behavior of atoms and the elementary particles and forces that compose them. No theory in the history of science has been more successful than quantum theory. It underlies our understanding of chemistry, atomic and subatomic physics, electronics and even biology.

In the same decades that quantum mechanics was being formulated, Albert Einstein constructed his general theory of relativity, which is a theory of gravity. In his theory, the gravitational force arises as a consequence of space and time (which together form "spacetime") being curved by the presence of matter. A loose analogy is that of a bowling ball placed on a rubber sheet along with a marble that is rolling around nearby. The balls could represent the sun and the earth, and the sheet is space. The bowling ball creates a deep indentation in the rubber sheet, and the slope of this indentation causes the marble to be deflected toward the larger ball, as if some force—gravity—were pulling it in that direction. Similarly, any piece of matter or concentration of energy distorts the geometry of spacetime, causing other particles and light rays to be deflected toward it, a phenomenon we call gravity.

Quantum theory and Einstein's theory of general relativity separately have each been fantastically well confirmed by experiment—but no experiment has explored the regime where both theories predict significant effects. The problem is that quantum effects are most prominent at small size scales, whereas general relativistic effects require large masses, so it takes extraordinary circumstances to combine both conditions.

Allied with this hole in the experimental data is a huge conceptual problem: Einstein's theory of general relativity is thoroughly classical, or nonquantum. For physics as a whole to be logically consistent, there has to be a theory that somehow unites quantum mechanics and general relativity. This long-sought-after theory is called quantum gravity. Because general relativity deals in the geometry of spacetime, a quantum theory of gravity will in addition be a quantum theory of spacetime.

Physicists have developed a considerable collection of mathematical procedures for turning a classical theory into a quantum one. Many theoretical physicists and mathematicians have worked on applying those standard techniques to general relativity. Early results were discouraging. Calculations carried out in the 1960s and 1970s seemed to show that quantum theory and

Overview/Quantum Spacetime

- To understand the structure of space on the very smallest size scale, we must turn to a quantum theory of gravity. Gravity is involved because Einstein's general theory of relativity reveals that gravity is caused by the warping of space and time.
- By carefully combining the fundamental principles of quantum mechanics and general relativity, physicists are led to the theory of "loop quantum gravity." In this theory, the allowed quantum states of space turn out to be related to diagrams of lines and nodes called spin networks. Quantum spacetime corresponds to similar diagrams called spin foams.
- Loop quantum gravity predicts that space comes in discrete lumps, the smallest of which is about a cubic Planck length, or 10^{-99} cubic centimeter. Time proceeds in discrete ticks of about a Planck time, or 10^{-43} second. The effects of this discrete structure might be seen in experiments in the near future.

general relativity could not be successfully combined. Consequently, something fundamentally new seemed to be required, such as additional postulates or principles not included in quantum theory and general relativity, or new particles or fields, or new entities of some kind. Perhaps with the right additions or a new mathematical structure, a quantumlike theory could be developed that would successfully approximate general relativity in the nonquantum regime. To avoid spoiling the successful predictions of quantum theory and general relativity, the exotica contained in the full theory would remain hidden from experiment except in the extraordinary circumstances where both quantum theory and general relativity are expected to have large effects. Many different approaches along these lines have been tried, with names such as twistor theory, noncommutative geometry and supergravity.

An approach that is very popular with physicists is string theory, which postulates that space has six or seven dimensions—all so far completely unobserved—in addition to the three that we are familiar with. String theory also predicts the existence of a great many new elementary particles and forces, for which there is so far no observable evidence. Some researchers believe that string theory is subsumed in a theory called M-theory [see "The Theory Formerly Known as Strings," by Michael J. Duff; *Scientific American*, February 1998], but unfortunately no precise definition of this conjectured theory has ever been given. Thus, many physicists and mathematicians are convinced that alternatives must be studied. Our loop quantum gravity theory is the best-developed alternative.

A Big Loophole

In the mid-1980s a few of us—including Abhay Ashtekar, now at Pennsylvania State University, Ted Jacobson of the University of Maryland and Carlo Rovelli, now at the University of the Mediterranean in Marseille—decided to reexamine the question of whether quantum mechanics could be combined consistently with general relativity using the standard techniques. We knew that the negative results from the 1970s had an important loophole. Those calculations assumed that the geometry of space is continuous and smooth, no matter how minutely we examine it, just as people had expected matter to be before the discovery of atoms. Some of our teachers and mentors had pointed out that if this assumption was wrong, the old calculations would not be reliable.

So we began searching for a way to do calculations without assuming that space is smooth and continuous. We insisted on not making any assumptions beyond the experimentally well tested principles of general relativity and quantum theory. In particular, we kept two key principles of general relativity at the heart of our calculations.

The first is known as background independence. This principle says that the geometry of spacetime is not fixed. Instead the geometry is an evolving, dynamical quantity. To find the geometry, one has to solve certain equations that include all the effects of matter and energy. Incidentally, string theory, as currently formulated, is not background independent; the equations describing the strings are set up in a predetermined classical (that is, nonquantum) spacetime.

The second principle, known by the imposing name diffeomorphism invariance, is closely related to background independence. This principle implies that, unlike theories prior to general relativity, one is free to choose any set of coordinates to map spacetime and express the equations. A point in spacetime is defined only by what physically happens at it, not by its location according to some special set of coordinates (no coordinates are special). Diffeomorphism invariance is very powerful and is of fundamental importance in general relativity.

By carefully combining these two principles with the standard techniques of quantum mechanics, we developed a mathematical language that allowed us to do a computation to determine whether space is continuous or discrete. That calculation revealed, to our delight, that space is quantized. We had laid the foundations of our theory of loop quantum gravity. The term "loop," by the way, arises from how some computations in the theory involve small loops marked out in spacetime.

The calculations have been redone by a number of physicists and mathematicians using a range of methods.

Over the years since, the study of loop quantum gravity has grown into a healthy field of research, with many contributors around the world; our combined efforts give us confidence in the picture of spacetime I will describe.

Ours is a quantum theory of the structure of space-time at the smallest size scales, so to explain how the theory works we need to consider what it predicts for a small region or volume. In dealing with quantum physics, it is essential to specify precisely what physical quantities are to be measured. To do so, we consider a region somewhere that is marked out by a boundary, B. The boundary may be defined by some matter, such as a cast-iron shell, or it may be defined by the geometry of spacetime itself, as in the event horizon of a black hole (a surface from within which even light cannot escape the black hole's gravitational clutches).

What happens if we measure the volume of the region? What are the possible outcomes allowed by both quantum theory and diffeomorphism invariance? If the geometry of space is continuous, the region could be of any size and the measurement result could be any positive real number; in particular, it could be as close as one wants to zero volume. But if the geometry is granular, then the measurement result can come from just a discrete set of numbers and it cannot be smaller than a certain minimum possible volume. The question is similar to asking how much energy electrons orbiting an atomic nucleus have. Classical mechanics predicts that that an electron can possess any amount of energy, but quantum mechanics allows only specific energies (amounts in between those values do not occur). The difference is like that between the measure of something that flows continuously, like the 19th-century conception of water, and something that can be counted, like the atoms in that water.

The theory of loop quantum gravity predicts that space is like atoms: there is a discrete set of numbers that the volume-measuring experiment can return. Volume comes in distinct pieces. Another quantity we can measure is the area of the boundary B. Again, calculations using the theory return an unambiguous result: the area of the surface is discrete as well. In other words, space is not continuous. It comes only in specific quantum units of area and volume.

The possible values of volume and area are measured in units of a quantity called the Planck length. This length is related to the strength of gravity, the size of quanta and the speed of light. It measures the scale at which the geometry of space is no longer continuous. The Planck length is very small: 10^{-33} centimeter. The smallest possible nonzero area is about a square Planck length, or 10^{-66} cm^2. The smallest nonzero volume is approximately a cubic Planck length, 10^{-99} cm^3. Thus, the theory predicts that there are about 10^{99} atoms of volume in every cubic centimeter of space. The quantum of volume is so tiny that there are more such quanta in a cubic centimeter than there are cubic centimeters in the visible universe (10^{85}).

Spin Networks

What else does our theory tell us about spacetime? To start with, what do these quantum states of volume and area look like? Is space made up of a lot of little cubes or spheres? The answer is no—it's not that simple. Nevertheless, we can draw diagrams that represent the quantum states of volume and area. To those of us working in this field, these diagrams are beautiful because of their connection to an elegant branch of mathematics.

To see how these diagrams work, imagine that we have a lump of space shaped like a cube. In our diagrams, we would depict this cube as a dot, which represents the volume, with six lines sticking out, each of which represents one of the cube's faces. We have to write a number next to the dot to specify the quantity of volume, and on each line we write a number to specify the area of the face that the line represents.

Next, suppose we put a pyramid on top of the cube. These two polyhedra, which share a common face, would be depicted as two dots (two volumes) connected by one of the lines (the face that joins the two volumes). The cube has five other faces (five lines sticking out), and the pyramid has four (four lines sticking out). It is clear how more complicated arrangements involving polyhedra other than cubes and pyramids could be depicted with these dot-and-line diagrams: each polyhedron of volume becomes a dot, or node, and each flat face of a poly-hedron becomes a line, and the lines join the nodes in the way that the faces join the polyhedra together. Mathematicians call these line diagrams graphs.

Now in our theory, we throw away the drawings of polyhedra and just keep the graphs. The mathematics that describes the quantum states of volume and area gives us a set of rules for how the nodes and lines can be connected and what numbers can go where in a diagram. Every quantum state corresponds to one of these graphs, and every graph that obeys the rules corresponds to a quantum state. The graphs are a convenient shorthand for all the possible quantum states of space. (The mathematics and other details of the quantum states are too complicated to discuss here; the best we can do is show some of the related diagrams.)

The graphs are a better representation of the quantum states than the polyhedra are. In particular, some graphs connect in strange ways that cannot be converted into a tidy picture of polyhedra. For example, whenever space is curved, the polyhedra will not fit together properly in any drawing we could do, yet we can still easily draw a graph. Indeed, we can take a graph and from it calculate how much space is distorted. Because the distortion of space is what produces gravity, this is how the diagrams form a quantum theory of gravity.

For simplicity, we often draw the graphs in two dimensions, but it is better to imagine them filling three-dimensional space, because that is what they represent. Yet there is a conceptual trap here: the lines and nodes of a graph do not live at specific locations in space. Each graph is defined only by the way its pieces connect together and how they relate to well-defined boundaries such as boundary B. The continuous, three-dimensional space that you are imagining the graphs occupy *does not exist* as a separate entity. All that exist are the lines and nodes; they *are* space, and the way they connect defines the geometry of space.

These graphs are called spin networks because the numbers on them are related to quantities called spins. Roger Penrose of the University of Oxford first proposed in the early 1970s that spin networks might play a role in theories of quantum gravity. We were very pleased when we found, in 1994, that precise calculations confirmed his intuition. Readers familiar with Feynman diagrams should note that our spin networks are *not* Feynman diagrams, despite the superficial resemblance. Feynman diagrams represent quantum interactions between particles, which proceed from one quantum state to another. Our diagrams represent fixed quantum states of spatial volumes and areas.

The individual nodes and edges of the diagrams represent extremely small regions of space: a node is typically a volume of about one cubic Planck length, and a line is typically an area of about one square Planck length. But in principle, nothing limits how big and complicated a spin network can be. If we could draw a detailed picture of the quantum state of our universe—the geometry of its space, as curved and warped by the gravitation of galaxies and black holes and everything else—it would be a gargantuan spin network of unimaginable complexity, with approximately 10^{184} nodes.

These spin networks describe the geometry of space. But what about all the matter and energy contained in that space? How do we represent particles and fields occupying positions and regions of space? Particles, such as electrons, correspond to certain types of nodes, which are represented by adding more labels on nodes. Fields, such as the electromagnetic field, are represented by additional labels on the lines of the graph. We represent particles and fields moving through space by these labels moving in discrete steps on the graphs.

Moves and Foams

Particles and fields are not the only things that move around. According to general relativity, the geometry of space changes in time. The bends and curves of space change as matter and energy move, and waves can pass through it like ripples on a lake [see "Ripples in Space and Time," by W. Wayt Gibbs; *Scientific American*, April 2002]. In loop quantum gravity, these processes are represented by changes in the graphs. They evolve in time by a succession of certain "moves" in which the connectivity of the graphs changes.

When physicists describe phenomena quantum-mechanically, they compute probabilities for different processes. We do the same when we apply loop quantum gravity theory to describe phenomena, whether it be particles and fields moving on the spin networks or the geometry of space itself evolving in time. In particular, Thomas Thiemann of the Perimeter Institute for Theoretical Physics in Waterloo, Ontario, has derived precise quantum probabilities for the spin network moves. With these the theory is completely specified: we have a well-defined procedure for computing the probability of any process that can occur in a world that obeys the rules of our theory. It remains only to do the computations and work out predictions for what could be observed in experiments of one kind or another.

Einstein's theories of special and general relativity join space and time together into the single, merged entity known as spacetime. The spin networks that represent space in loop quantum gravity theory accommodate the concept of spacetime by becoming what we call spin "foams." With the addition of another dimension—time—the lines of the spin networks grow to become two-dimensional surfaces, and the nodes grow to become lines. Transitions where the spin networks change (the moves discussed earlier) are now represented by nodes where the lines meet in the foam. The spin foam picture of spacetime was proposed by several people, including Carlo Rovelli, Mike Reisenberger (now of the University of Montevideo), John Barrett of the University of Nottingham, Louis Crane of Kansas State University, John Baez of the University of California at Riverside and Fotini Markopoulou of the Perimeter Institute for Theoretical Physics.

In the spacetime way of looking at things, a snapshot at a specific time is like a slice cutting across the spacetime. Taking such a slice through a spin foam produces a spin network. But it would be wrong to think of such a slice as moving continuously, like a smooth flow of time. Instead, just as space is defined by a spin network's discrete geometry, time is defined by the sequence of distinct moves that rearrange the network. In this way time also becomes discrete. Time flows not like a river but like the ticking of a clock, with "ticks" that are about as long as the Planck time: 10^{-43} second. Or, more precisely, time in our universe flows by the ticking of innumerable clocks—in a sense, at every location in the spin foam where a quantum "move" takes place, a clock at that location has ticked once.

Predictions and Tests

I have outlined what loop quantum gravity has to say about space and time at the Planck scale, but we cannot verify the theory directly by examining spacetime on that scale. It is too small. So how can we test the theory? An important test is whether one can derive classical general relativity as an approximation to loop quantum gravity. In other words, if the spin networks are like the threads woven into a piece of cloth, this is analogous to asking whether we can compute the right elastic properties for a sheet of the material by averaging over thousands of threads. Similarly, when averaged over many Planck lengths, do spin networks describe the geometry of space and its evolution in a way that agrees roughly with the "smooth cloth" of Einstein's classical theory? This is a difficult problem, but recently researchers have made progress for some cases, for certain configurations of the material, so to speak. For example, long-wavelength gravitational waves propagating on otherwise flat (uncurved) space can be described as excitations of specific quantum states described by the loop quantum gravity theory.

Another fruitful test is to see what loop quantum gravity has to say about one of the long-standing mysteries of gravitational physics and quantum theory: the thermodynamics of black holes, in particular their entropy, which is related to disorder. Physicists have computed predictions regarding black hole thermo-dynamics using a hybrid, approximate theory in which matter is treated quantum-mechanically but spacetime is not. A full quantum theory of gravity, such as loop quantum gravity, should be able to reproduce these predictions. Specifically, in the 1970s Jacob D. Bekenstein, now at the Hebrew University of Jerusalem, inferred that black holes must be ascribed an entropy proportional to their surface area [see "Information in the Holographic Universe," by Jacob D. Bekenstein;

Scientific American, August 2003]. Shortly after, Stephen Hawking deduced that black holes, particularly small ones, must emit radiation. These predictions are among the greatest results of theoretical physics in the past 30 years.

To do the calculation in loop quantum gravity, we pick the boundary B to be the event horizon of a black hole. When we analyze the entropy of the relevant quantum states, we get *precisely* the prediction of Bekenstein. Similarly, the theory reproduces Hawking's prediction of black hole radiation. In fact, it makes further predictions for the fine structure of Hawking radiation. If a microscopic black hole is ever observed, this prediction could be tested by studying the spectrum of radiation it emits. That may be far off in time, however, because we have no technology to make black holes, small or otherwise.

Indeed, any experimental test of loop quantum gravity would appear at first to be an immense techno-logical challenge. The problem is that the characteristic effects described by the theory become significant only at the Planck scale, the very tiny size of the quanta of area and volume. The Planck scale is 16 orders of magnitude below the scale probed in the highest-energy particle accelerators currently planned (higher energy is needed to probe shorter distance scales). Because we cannot reach the Planck scale with an accelerator, many people have held out little hope for the confirmation of quantum gravity theories.

In the past several years, however, a few imaginative young researchers have thought up new ways to test the predictions of loop quantum gravity that can be done now. These methods depend on the propagation of light across the universe. When light moves through a medium, its wavelength suffers some distortions, leading to effects such as bending in water and the separation of different wavelengths, or colors. These effects also occur for light and particles moving through the discrete space described by a spin network.

Unfortunately, the magnitude of the effects is proportional to the ratio of the Planck length to the wavelength. For visible light, this ratio is smaller than 10^{-28}; even for the most powerful cosmic rays ever observed, it is about one billionth. For any radiation we can observe, the effects of the granular structure of space are very small. What the young researchers spotted is that these effects accumulate when light travels a long distance. And we detect light and particles that come from billions of light years away, from events such as gamma-ray bursts [see "The Brightest Explosions in the Universe," by Neil Gehrels, Luigi Piro and Peter J. T. Leonard; *Scientific American*, December 2002].

A gamma-ray burst spews out photons in a range of energies in a very brief explosion. Calculations in loop quantum gravity, by Rodolfo Gambini of the University of the Republic in Uruguay, Jorge Pullin of Louisiana State University and others, predict that photons of different energies should travel at slightly different speeds and therefore arrive at slightly different times. We can look for this effect in data from satellite observations of gamma-ray bursts. So far the precision is about a factor of 1,000 below what is needed, but a new satellite observatory called GLAST, planned for 2006, will have the precision required.

The reader may ask if this result would mean that Einstein's theory of special relativity is wrong when it predicts a universal speed of light. Several people, including Giovanni Amelino-Camelia of the University of Rome "La Sapienza" and João Magueijo of Imperial College London, as well as myself, have developed modified versions of Einstein's theory that will accommodate high-energy photons traveling at different speeds. Our theories propose that the universal speed is the speed of very low energy photons or, equivalently, long-wavelength light.

Another possible effect of discrete spacetime involves very high energy cosmic rays. More than 30 years ago researchers predicted that cosmic-ray protons with an energy greater than 3×10^{19} electron volts would scatter off the cosmic microwave background that fills space and should therefore never reach the earth. Puzzlingly, a Japanese experiment called AGASA has detected more than 10 cosmic rays with an energy over this limit. But it turns out that the discrete structure of space can raise the energy required for the scattering reaction, allowing higher-energy cosmic-ray protons to reach the earth. If the AGASA observations hold up, and if no other explanation is found, then it may turn out that we have already detected the discreteness of space.

The Cosmos

In addition to making predictions about specific phenomena such as high-energy cosmic rays, loop quantum gravity has opened up a new window through which we can study deep cosmological questions such as those relating to the origins of our universe. We can use the theory to study the earliest moments of time just after the big bang. General relativity predicts that there was a first moment of time, but this conclusion ignores quantum physics (because general relativity is not a quantum theory). Recent loop quantum gravity calculations by Martin Bojowald of the Max Planck Institute for Gravitational Physics in Golm, Germany, indicate that the big bang is actually a big bounce; before the bounce the universe was rapidly contracting. Theorists are now hard at work developing predictions for the early universe that may be testable in future cosmological observations. It is not impossible that in our lifetime we could see evidence of the time before the big bang.

A question of similar profundity concerns the cosmological constant—a positive or negative energy density that could permeate "empty" space. Recent observations of distant supernovae and the cosmic microwave background strongly indicate that this energy does exist and is positive, which accelerates the universe's expansion [see "The Quintessential Universe," by Jeremiah P. Ostriker and Paul J. Steinhardt; *Scientific American*, January 2001]. Loop quantum gravity has no trouble incorporating the positive energy density. This fact was demonstrated in 1990, when Hideo Kodama of Kyoto University wrote down equations describing an exact quantum state of a universe having a positive cosmological constant.

Many open questions remain to be answered in loop quantum gravity. Some are technical matters that need to be clarified. We would also like to understand how, if at all, special relativity must be modified at extremely high energies. So far our speculations on this topic are not solidly linked to loop quantum gravity calculations. In addition, we would like to know that classical general relativity is a good approximate description of the theory for distances much larger than the Planck length, in all circumstances. (At present we know only that the approximation is good for certain states that describe rather weak gravitational waves propagating on an otherwise flat spacetime.) Finally, we would like to understand whether or not loop quantum gravity has anything to say about unification: Are the different forces, including gravity, all aspects of a single, funda-mental force? String theory is based on a particular idea about unification, but we also have ideas for achieving unification with loop quantum gravity.

Loop quantum gravity occupies a very important place in the development of physics. It is arguably *the* quantum theory of general relativity, because it makes no extra assumptions beyond the basic principles of quantum theory and relativity theory. The remarkable departure that it makes—proposing a discontinuous spacetime described by spin networks and spin foam— emerges from the mathematics of the theory itself, rather than being inserted as an ad hoc postulate.

Still, everything I have discussed is theoretical. It could be that in spite of all I have described here, space really is continuous, no matter how small the scale we probe. Then physicists would have to turn to more radical postulates, such as those of string theory. Because this is science, in the end experiment will decide. The good news is that the decision may come soon.

More to Explore

Three Roads to Quantum Gravity. Lee Smolin. Basic Books, 2001.

The Quantum of Area? John Baez in *Nature*, Vol. 421, pages 702–703; February 2003.

How Far Are We from the Quantum Theory of Gravity? Lee Smolin. March 2003. Preprint available at **http://arxiv.org/hep-th/0303185.**

Welcome to Quantum Gravity. Special section. *Physics World*, Vol. 16, No. 11, pages 27–50; November 2003.

Loop Quantum Gravity. Lee Smolin. Online at **www. edge.org/3rd–culture/smolin03/smolin03–index.html.**

About the Author

LEE SMOLIN is a researcher at the Perimeter Institute for Theoretical Physics in Waterloo, Ontario, and an adjunct professor of physics at the University of Waterloo. He has a B.A. from Hampshire College and a Ph.D. from Harvard University and has been on the faculty of Yale, Syracuse and Pennsylvania State universities. In addition to his work on quantum gravity, he is interested in elementary particle physics, cosmology and the foundations of quantum theory. His 1997 book, The Life of the Cosmos (Oxford University Press), explored the philosophical implications of developments in contemporary physics and cosmology.

7. "The Dawn of Physics Beyond the Standard Model"

By Gordon Kane

The Standard Model of particle physics is at a pivotal moment in its
history: It is both at the height of its success
and on the verge of being surpassed.

Today, centuries after the search began for the fundamental constituents that make up all the complexity and
beauty of the everyday world, we have an astonishingly
simple answer—it takes just six particles: the electron,
the up and the down quarks, the gluon, the photon and
the Higgs boson. Eleven additional particles suffice to
describe all the esoteric phenomena studied by particle
physicists [see "The Standard Model" box]. This is not
speculation akin to the ancient Greeks' four elements
of earth, air, water and fire. Rather it is a conclusion
embodied in the most sophisticated mathematical theory
of nature in history, the Standard Model of particle
physics. Despite the word "model" in its name, the
Standard Model is a comprehensive theory that identifies
the basic particles and specifies how they interact.
Everything that happens in our world (except for the
effects of gravity) results from Standard Model particles
interacting according to its rules and equations.

The Standard Model was formulated in the 1970s
and tentatively established by experiments in the early
1980s. Nearly three decades of exacting experiments

Overview/A New Era

- The Standard Model of particle physics is the most successful theory of nature in history, but increasingly there are signs that it must be extended by adding new particles that play roles in high-energy reactions.
- Major experiments are on the verge of providing direct evidence of these new particles. After 30 years of consolidation, particle physics is entering a new era of discovery. Many profound mysteries could be resolved by post–Standard Model physics.
- One element of the Standard Model—a particle called the Higgs boson—also remains to be observed. The Tevatron collider at Fermilab could detect Higgs bosons within the next few years.

have tested and verified the theory in meticulous detail, confirming all of its predictions. In one respect, this success is rewarding because it confirms that we really understand, at a deeper level than ever before, how nature works. Paradoxically, the success has also been frustrating. Before the advent of the Standard Model, physicists had become used to experiments producing unexpected new particles or other signposts to a new theory almost before the chalk dust had settled on the old one. They have been waiting 30 years for that to happen with the Standard Model.

Their wait should soon be over. Experiments that achieve collisions that are higher in energy than ever before or that study certain key phenomena with greater precision are on the verge of going beyond the Standard Model. These results will not overturn the Standard Model. Instead they will extend it by uncovering particles and forces not described by it. The most important experiment is occurring at the upgraded Tevatron collider at Fermi National Accelerator

Laboratory in Batavia, Ill., which began taking data in 2001. It might produce directly the still elusive particles that complete the Standard Model (Higgs bosons) and those predicted by the most compelling extensions of the theory (the so-called superpartners of the known particles).

Significant information is also beginning to come from "B factories," particle colliders running in California and Japan configured to create billions of b quarks (one of the 11 additional particles) and their antimatter equivalents to study a phenomenon called CP violation. CP (charge-parity) is the symmetry relating matter to antimatter, and CP violation means that antimatter does not exactly mirror matter in its behavior. The amount of CP violation observed so far in particle decays can be accommodated by the Standard Model, but we have reasons to expect much more CP violation than it can produce. Physics that goes beyond the Standard Model can generate additional CP violation.

Physicists are also studying the precise electric and magnetic properties of particles. The Standard Model predicts that electrons and quarks behave as microscopic magnets with a specific strength and that their behavior in an electric field is determined purely by their electric charge. Most extensions of the Standard Model predict a slightly different magnetic strength and electrical behavior. Experiments are beginning to collect data with enough sensitivity to see the tiny effects predicted.

The Standard Model

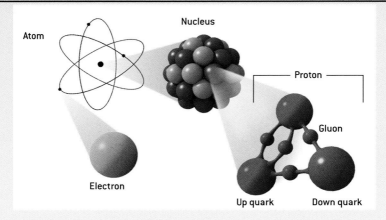

The Particles

Although the Standard Model needs to be extended, its particles suffice to describe the everyday world (except for gravity) and almost all data collected by particle physicists.

MATTER PARTICLES (FERMIONS) In the Standard Model, the fundamental particles of ordinary matter are the electron, the up quark (u) and the down quark (d). Triplets of quarks bind together to form protons (uud) and neutrons (udd), which in turn make up atomic nuclei (*above*). The electron and the up and the down quarks, together with the electron-neutrino, form the first of three groups of particles called generations. Each generation is identical in every respect except for the masses of the particles (*grid at right*). The values of the neutrino masses in the chart are speculative but chosen to be consistent with observations.

FORCE CARRIERS (BOSONS) The Standard Model describes three of the four known forces: electromagnetism, the weak force (which is involved in the formation of the chemical elements) and the strong force (which holds protons, neutrons and nuclei together). The forces are mediated by force particles: photons for electromagnetism, the W and Z bosons for the weak force, and gluons for the strong force. For gravity, gravitons are postulated, but the Standard Model does not include gravity. The Standard Model partially unifies the electromagnetic and weak forces—they are facets of one "electroweak" force at high energies or, equivalently, at distances smaller than the diameter of protons.

One of the greatest successes of the Standard Model is that the forms of the forces—the detailed structure of the equations describing them—are largely determined by general principles embodied in the theory rather than being chosen in an ad hoc fashion to match a collection of empirical data. For electromagnetism, for example, the validity of relativistic quantum field theory (on which the Standard Model is based) and the existence of the electron imply that the photon must also exist and interact in the way that it does— we finally understand light. Similar arguments predicted the existence and properties, later confirmed, of gluons and the W and Z particles.

THE SOURCE OF MASS In addition to the particles described above, the Standard Model predicts the existence of the Higgs boson, which has not yet been directly detected by experiment. The Higgs interacts with the other particles in a special manner that gives them mass.

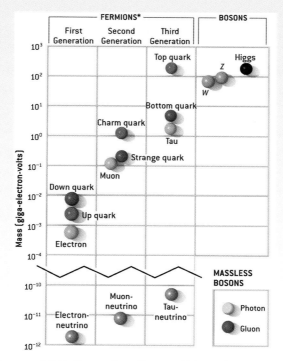

*The fermions are subdivided into quarks and leptons, with leptons including electrons, muons, taus and three forms of neutrino.

(continued next page)

The Standard Model (continued)

DEEPER LEVELS? Might the Standard Model be superseded by a theory in which quarks and electrons are made up of more fundamental particles? Almost certainly not. Experiments have probed much more deeply than ever before without finding a hint of additional structure. More important, the Standard Model is a consistent theory that makes sense if electrons and quarks are fundamental. There are no loose ends hinting at a deeper underlying structure. Further, all the forces become similar at high energies, particularly if super-symmetry is true [see "Evidence for Supersymmetry" box]. If electrons and quarks are composite, this unification fails: the forces do not become equal. Relativistic quantum field theory views electrons and quarks as being pointlike—they are structureless. In the future, they might be thought of as tiny strings or membranes (as in string theory), but they will still be electrons and quarks, with all the known Standard Model properties of these objects at low energies.

The Rules of the Game

The Standard Model describes the fundamental particles and how they interact. For a full understanding of nature, we also need to know what rules to use to calculate the results of the interactions. An example that helps to elucidate this point is Newton's law, $F = ma$. F is any force, m is the mass of any particle, and a is the acceleration of the particle induced by the force. Even if you know the particles and the forces acting on them, you cannot calculate how the particles behave unless you also know the rule $F = ma$. The modern version of the rules is relativistic quantum field theory, which was invented in the first half of the 20th century. In the second half of the 20th century the development of the Standard Model taught researchers about the nature of the particles and forces that were playing by the rules of quantum field theory. The classical concept of a force is also extended by the Standard Model: in addition to pushing and pulling on one another, when particles interact they can change their identity and be created or destroyed.

Feynman diagrams (*a–g, at right*), first devised by physicist Richard P. Feynman, serve as useful shorthand to describe interactions in quantum field theory. The straight lines represent the trajectories of matter particles; the wavy lines represent those of force particles. Electromagnetism is produced by the emission or absorption of photons by any charged particle, such as an electron or a quark. In a, the incoming electron emits a photon and travels off in a new direction. The strong force involves gluons emitted (b) or absorbed by quarks. The weak force involves W and Z particles (c, d), which are emitted or absorbed by both quarks and leptons (electrons, muons, taus and neutrinos). Notice how the W causes the electron to change identity. Gluons (e) and Ws and Zs (f) also self-interact, but photons do not.

Diagrams a through f are called interaction vertices. Forces are produced by combining two or more vertices. For example, the electromagnetic force between an electron and a quark is largely generated by the transfer of a photon (g). *Everything* that happens in our world, except for gravity, is the result of combinations of these vertices. —G. K.

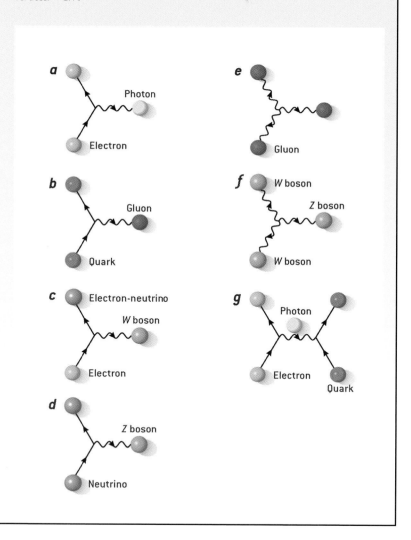

Looking beyond the earth, scientists studying solar neutrinos and cosmic-ray neutrinos, ghostly particles that barely interact at all, have recently established that neutrinos have masses, a result long expected by theorists studying extensions of the Standard Model [see "Solving the Solar Neutrino Problem," by Arthur B. McDonald, Joshua R. Klein and David L. Wark; *Scientific American*, April]. The next round of experiments will clarify the form of theory needed to explain the observed neutrino masses.

In addition, experiments are under way to detect mysterious particles that form the cold dark matter of the universe and to examine protons at higher levels of sensitivity to learn whether they decay. Success in either project would be a landmark of post–Standard Model physics.

As all this research proceeds, it is ushering in a new, data-rich era in particle physics. Joining the fray by about 2007 will be the Large Hadron Collider (LHC), a machine 27 kilometers in circumference now under construction at CERN, the European laboratory for particle physics near Geneva [see "The Large Hadron Collider," by Chris Llewellyn Smith; *Scientific American*, July 2000]. A 30-kilometer-long linear electron-positron collider that will complement the LHC's results is in the design stages.

As the first hints of post–Standard Model physics are glimpsed, news reports often make it sound as if the Standard Model has been found to be wrong, as if it were broken and ready to be discarded, but that is not the right way to think about it. Take the example of Maxwell's equations, written down in the late 19th century to describe the electromagnetic force. In the early 20th century we learned that at atomic sizes a quantum version of Maxwell's equations is needed. Later the Standard Model included these quantum Maxwell's equations as a subset of its equations. In neither case do we say Maxwell's equations are wrong. They are extended. (And they are still used to design innumerable electronic technologies.)

A Permanent Edifice

Similarly, the standard model is here to stay. It is a full mathematical theory—a multiply connected and highly stable edifice. It will turn out to be one piece of a larger such edifice, but it cannot be "wrong." No part of the theory can fail without a collapse of the entire structure. If the theory were wrong, many successful tests would be accidents. It will continue to describe strong, weak and electromagnetic interactions at low energies.

The Standard Model is very well tested. It predicted the existence of the W and Z bosons, the gluon and two of the heavier quarks (the charm and the top quark). All these particles were subsequently found, with precisely the predicted properties.

A second major test involves the electroweak mixing angle, a parameter that plays a role in describing the

Evidence for Supersymmetry

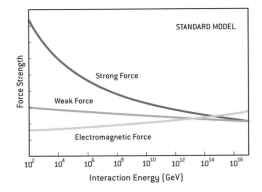

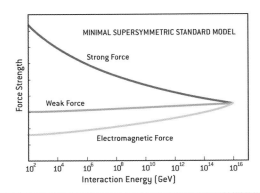

The most widely favored theory to supersede the Standard Model is the Minimal Supersymmetric Standard Model. In this model, every known particle species has a superpartner particle that is related to it by supersymmetry. Particles come in two broad classes: bosons (such as the force particles), which can gather en masse in a single state, and fermions (such as quarks and leptons), which avoid having identical states. The superpartner of a fermion is always a boson and vice versa.

Indirect evidence for supersymmetry comes from the extrapolation of interactions to high energies. In the Standard Model, the three forces become similar but not equal in strength (*top*). The existence of superpartners changes the extrapolation so that the forces all coincide at one energy (*bottom*)—a clue that they become unified if supersymmetry is true.

weak and electromagnetic interactions. That mixing angle must have the same value for every electroweak process. If the Standard Model were wrong, the mixing angle could have one value for one process, a different value for another and so on. It is observed to have the same value everywhere, to an accuracy of about 1 percent.

Third, the Large Electron-Positron (LEP) collider at CERN, which ran from 1989 to 2000, looked at about 20 million Z bosons. Essentially every one of them decayed in the manner expected by the Standard Model, which predicted the number of instances of each kind of decay as well as details of the energies and directions of the outgoing particles. These tests are but a few of the many that have solidly confirmed the Standard Model.

In its full glory, the Standard Model has 17 particles and about as many free parameters—quantities such as particle masses and strengths of interactions [see "The Standard Model" box]. These quantities can in principle take any value, and we learn the correct values only by making measurements. Armchair critics sometimes compare the Standard Model's many parameters with the epicycles on epicycles that medieval theorists used to describe planetary orbits. They imagine that the Standard Model has limited predictive power, or that its content is arbitrary, or that it can explain anything by adjusting of some parameter.

The opposite is actually true: once the masses and interaction strengths are measured in any process, they are fixed for the whole theory and for any other experiment, leaving no freedom at all. Moreover, the detailed forms of all the Standard Model's equations are determined by the theory. Every parameter but the Higgs boson mass has been measured. Until we go beyond the Standard Model, the only thing that can change with new results is the precision of our knowledge of the parameters, and as that improves it becomes harder, not easier, for all the experimental data to remain consistent, because measured quantities must agree to higher levels of precision.

Adding further particles and interactions to extend the Standard Model might seem to introduce a lot more freedom, but this is not necessarily the case. The most widely favored extension is the Minimal Supersymmetric Standard Model (MSSM). Supersymmetry assigns a superpartner particle to every particle species. We know little about the masses of those superpartners, but their interactions are constrained by the supersymmetry. Once the masses are measured, the predictions of the MSSM will be even more tightly constrained than the Standard Model because of the mathematical relations of supersymmetry.

Ten Mysteries

If the standard model works so well, why must it be extended? A big hint arises when we pursue the long-standing goal of unifying the forces of nature. In the

Standard Model, we can extrapolate the forces and ask how they would behave at much higher energies. For example, what were the forces like in the extremely high temperatures extant soon after the big bang? At low energies the strong force is about 30 times as powerful as the weak force and more than 100 times as powerful as electromagnetism. When we extrapolate, we find that the strengths of these three forces become very similar but are never all exactly the same. If we extend the Standard Model to the MSSM, the forces become essentially identical at a specific high energy [see "Evidence of Supersymmetry" box]. Even better, the gravitational force approaches the same strength at a slightly higher energy, suggesting a connection between the Standard Model forces and gravity. These results seem like strong clues in favor of the MSSM.

Other reasons for extending the Standard Model arise from phenomena it cannot explain or cannot even accommodate:

1. All our theories today seem to imply that the universe should contain a tremendous concentration of energy, even in the emptiest regions of space. The gravitational effects of this so-called vacuum energy would have either quickly curled up the universe long ago or expanded it to much greater size. The Standard Model cannot help us under stand this puzzle, called the cosmological constant problem.

2. The expansion of the universe was long believed to be slowing down because of the mutual gravitational attraction of all the matter in the universe. We now know that the expansion is accelerating and that whatever causes the acceleration (dubbed "dark energy") cannot be Standard Model physics.

3. There is very good evidence that in the first fraction of a second of the big bang the universe went through a stage of extremely rapid expansion called inflation. The fields responsible for inflation cannot be Standard Model ones.

4. If the universe began in the big bang as a huge burst of energy, it should have evolved into equal parts matter and antimatter (CP symmetry). But instead the stars and nebulae are made of protons, neutrons and electrons and not their antiparticles (their antimatter equivalents). This matter asymmetry cannot be explained by the Standard Model.

5. About a quarter of the universe is invisible cold dark matter that cannot be particles of the Standard Model.

6. In the Standard Model, interactions with the Higgs field (which is associated with the Higgs boson) cause particles to have mass. The Standard Model

cannot explain the very special forms that the Higgs interactions must take.

7. Quantum corrections apparently make the calculated Higgs boson mass huge, which in turn would make all particle masses huge. That result cannot be avoided in the Standard Model and thus causes a serious conceptual problem.

8. The Standard Model cannot include gravity, because it does not have the same structure as the other three forces.

9. The values of the masses of the quarks and leptons (such as the electron and neutrinos) cannot be explained by the Standard Model.

10. The Standard Model has three "generations" of particles. The everyday world is made up entirely of first-generation particles, and that generation appears to form a consistent theory on its own. The Standard Model describes all three generations, but it cannot explain why more than one exists.

In expressing these mysteries, when I say the Standard Model cannot explain a given phenomenon, I do not mean that the theory has not yet explained it but might do so one day. The Standard Model is a highly constrained theory, and it cannot ever explain the phenomena listed above. Possible explanations do exist. One reason the supersymmetric extension is attractive to many physicists is that it can address all but the second and the last three of these mysteries. String theory (in which particles are represented by tiny, one-dimensional entities instead of point objects) addresses the last three [see "The Theory Formerly Known as Strings," by Michael J. Duff; *Scientific American*, February 1998]. The phenomena that the Standard Model cannot explain are clues to how it will be extended.

It is not surprising that there are questions that the Standard Model cannot answer—every successful theory in science has increased the number of answered questions but has left some unanswered. And even though improved understanding has led to new questions that could not be formulated earlier, the number of unanswered fundamental questions has continued to decrease.

Some of these 10 mysteries demonstrate another reason why particle physics today is entering a new era. It has become clear that many of the deepest problems in cosmology have their solutions in particle physics, so the fields have merged into "particle cosmology." Only from cosmological studies could we learn that the universe is matter (and not antimatter) or that the universe is about a quarter cold dark matter. Any theoretical understanding of these phenomena must explain how they arise as part of the evolution of the universe after the big bang. But cosmology alone cannot tell us what particles make up cold dark matter, or how the matter asymmetry is actually generated, or how inflation originates. Understanding of the largest and the smallest phenomena must come together.

The Higgs

Physicists are tackling all these post–Standard Model mysteries, but one essential aspect of the Standard Model also remains to be completed. To give mass to leptons, quarks, and W and Z bosons, the theory relies on the Higgs field, which has not yet been directly detected.

The Higgs is fundamentally unlike any other field. To understand how it is different, consider the electromagnetic field. Electric charges give rise to electro-magnetic fields such as those all around us (just turn on a radio to sense them). Electromagnetic fields carry energy. A region of space has its lowest possible energy when the electromagnetic field vanishes throughout it. Zero field is the natural state in the absence of charged particles. Surprisingly, the Standard Model requires that the lowest energy occur when the Higgs field has a specific nonzero value. Consequently, a nonzero Higgs field permeates the universe, and particles always interact with this field, traveling through it like people wading through water. The interaction gives them their mass, their inertia.

Associated with the Higgs field is the Higgs boson. In the Standard Model, we cannot predict any particle masses from first principles, including the mass of the Higgs boson itself. One can, however, use other measured quantities to calculate some masses, such as those of the W and Z bosons and the top quark. Those predictions are confirmed, giving assurance to the underlying Higgs physics.

Physicists do already know something about the Higgs mass. Experimenters at the LEP collider measured about 20 quantities that are related to one another by the Standard Model. All the parameters needed to calculate predictions for those quantities are already measured—except for the Higgs boson mass. One can therefore work backward from the data and ask which Higgs mass gives the best fit to the 20 quantities. The answer is that the Higgs mass is less than about 200 giga-electron-volts (GeV). (The proton mass is about 0.9 GeV; the top quark 174 GeV.) That there is an answer at all is strong evidence that the Higgs exists. If the Higgs did not exist and the Standard Model were wrong, it would take a remarkable coincidence for the 20 quantities to be related in the right way to be consistent with a specific Higgs mass. Our confidence in this procedure is bolstered because a similar approach accurately predicted the top quark mass before any top quarks had been detected directly.

LEP also conducted a direct search for Higgs particles, but it could search only up to a mass of about 115 GeV. At that very upper limit of LEP's reach, a small number of events involved particles that behaved as Higgs bosons should. But there were not enough data to be sure a Higgs boson was actually discovered. Together the results suggest the Higgs mass lies between 115 and 200 GeV.

LEP is now dismantled to make way for the construction of the LHC, which is scheduled to begin taking data in four years. In the meantime the search for the Higgs continues at the Tevatron at Fermilab. If the Tevatron operates at its design intensity and energy and does not lose running time because of technical or funding difficulties, it could confirm the 115-GeV Higgs boson in about two to three years. If the Higgs is heavier, it will take longer for a clear signal to emerge from the background. The Tevatron will produce more than 10,000 Higgs bosons altogether if it runs as planned, and it could test whether the Higgs boson behaves as predicted. The LHC will be a "factory" for Higgs bosons, producing millions of them and allowing extensive studies.

There are also good arguments that some of the lighter superpartner particles predicted by the MSSM have masses small enough so that they could be produced at the Tevatron as well. Direct confirmation of supersymmetry could come in the next few years. The lightest superpartner is a prime candidate to make up the cold dark matter of the universe—it could be directly observed for the first time by the Tevatron. The LHC will produce large numbers of superpartners if they exist, definitively testing whether supersymmetry is part of nature.

Effective Theories

To fully grasp the relation of the Standard Model to the rest of physics, and its strengths and limitations, it is useful to think in terms of effective theories. An effective theory is a description of an aspect of nature that has inputs that are, in principle at least, calculable using a deeper theory. For example, in nuclear physics one takes the mass, charge and spin of the proton as inputs. In the Standard Model, one can calculate those quantities, using properties of quarks and gluons as inputs. Nuclear physics is an effective theory of nuclei, whereas the Standard Model is the effective theory of quarks and gluons.

From this point of view, every effective theory is open-ended and equally fundamental—that is, not truly fundamental at all. Will the ladder of effective theories continue? The MSSM solves a number of problems the Standard Model does not solve, but it is also an effective theory because it has inputs as well. Its inputs might be calculable in string theory.

Even from the perspective of effective theories, particle physics may have special status. Particle physics might increase our understanding of nature to the point where the theory can be formulated with no inputs. String theory or one of its cousins might allow the calculation of all inputs—not only the electron mass and such quantities but also the existence of space-time and the rules of quantum theory. But we are still an effective theory or two away from achieving that goal.

More to Explore

The Particle Garden. Gordon Kane. Perseus Publishing, 1996.

The Rise of the Standard Model: A History of Particle Physics from 1964 to 1979. Edited by Lillian Hoddeson, Laurie M. Brown, Michael Riordan and Max Dresden. Cambridge University Press, 1997.

The Little Book of the Big Bang: A Cosmic Primer. Craig J. Hogan. Copernicus Books, 1998.

Supersymmetry: Unveiling the Ultimate Laws of Nature. Gordon Kane. Perseus Publishing, 2001.

An excellent collection of particle physics Web sites is listed at **particleadventure.org/particleadventure/ other/othersites.html.**

About the Author

GORDON KANE, a particle theorist, is Victor Weisskopf Collegiate Professor of Physics at the University of Michigan at Ann Arbor. His work explores ways to test and extend the Standard Model of particle physics. In particular he studies Higgs physics and the Standard Model's supersymmetric extension, with a focus on relating theory and experiment and on the implications of supersymmetry for particle physics and cosmology. His hobbies include playing squash, exploring the history of ideas, and seeking to understand why science flourishes in some cultures but not others.

WEB SITES

Due to the changing nature of Internet links, Rosen Publishing has developed an online list of Web sites related to the subject of this book. This site is updated regularly. Please use this link to access the list:

http://www.rosenlinks.com/saces/exph

For Further Reading

Greene, Brian. *The Elegant Universe: Superstrings, Hidden Dimensions, and the Quest for the Ultimate Theory.* New York, NY: Vintage, 2000.

Greene, Brian. *The Fabric of the Cosmos: Space, Time, and the Texture of Reality.* New York, NY: Vintage, 2005.

Kaku, Michio. *Hyperspace: A Scientific Odyssey Through Parallel Universes, Time Warps, and the 10th Dimension.* New York, NY: Anchor, 1995.

Thorne, Kip S. *Black Holes and Time Warps: Einstein's Outrageous Legacy.* New York, NY: W. W. Norton & Company, 1995.

Tyson, Neil deGrasse. *Death by Black Hole: And Other Cosmic Quandaries.* New York, NY: W. W. Norton & Company, 2007.

Wolf, Fred Alan. *Parallel Universes.* New York, NY: Simon & Schuster, 1990.

INDEX